# WHITEHEAD'S PHILOSOPHY
## OF ORGANISM

# WHITEHEAD'S
# PHILOSOPHY OF ORGANISM

BY

## DOROTHY EMMET

PROFESSOR OF PHILOSOPHY IN THE UNIVERSITY OF MANCHESTER
HONORARY FELLOW OF LADY MARGARET HALL, OXFORD

*Second Edition*

## MACMILLAN
London · Melbourne · Toronto

## ST MARTIN'S PRESS
New York

1966

© Dorothy Emmet 1966

*First Edition* 1932
*Second Edition* 1966




MACMILLAN AND COMPANY LIMITED
*Little Essex Street London WC* 2
*also Bombay Calcutta Madras Melbourne*

THE MACMILLAN COMPANY OF CANADA LIMITED
*70 Bond Street Toronto* 2

ST MARTIN'S PRESS INC
*175 Fifth Avenue New York NY* 10010



Library of Congress Catalogue Card No. 66-19867




PRINTED IN GREAT BRITAIN BY
LOWE AND BRYDONE (PRINTERS) LTD., LONDON, N.W. 10

IN MEMORY OF
MY FATHER,
"A FELLOW-WORKER
WITH THE TRUTH."

# CONTENTS

a limitation amid alternative possibilities. Metaphysical status of these relevant possibilities.
The Primordial Nature of God. Difficulty in
using the name " God " in this connection.
Abstractive hierarchies. Subjective and objective eternal objects. Comparison with some
discussions in the *Sophist*.

An act of experience as a construction. White-
head's philosophy " a critique of pure feeling."
Does it involve a " pathetic fallacy "? The
Categorical Obligations. Distinction between
physical and conceptual feelings. Hybrid feel-
ings. The transmission of feelings. Theory of
Perception. Causal efficacy and Presentational
Immediacy. Theory of Propositions, and
Judgments. " Metaphysical propositions."

Problem of the formal elements in concrete
fact. Atomism and organism. Relation of
atomic actual entities to organic nexūs ; and to
former view of objects and events. Cellular
theory. Enduring objects ; societies of actual
entities. Order and novelty. The Extensive
Continuum. Properties of Extensive Connection. The Method of Extensive Abstraction. Systematic uniformities as presuppositions of Induction and Measurement. Laws of
nature. Morphology of evolution in types of
order. " Living " organisms. The Order of
Reason.

# PREFACE TO THE SECOND EDITION

THIS book on Whitehead's metaphysical philosophy was first published in 1932 and has been long out of print. Up to now I have resisted requests for a paperback reprint, on the grounds that since 1932 a good deal more and better work on the interpretation of Whitehead has been done by other people. Also this was a juvenile work insufficiently critical by my own standards, let alone those of others. Now, however, I have allowed myself to be persuaded, whether rightly or wrongly, that the book still interests people, and might be republished. If it is still of interest it may be because it conveys the intellectual excitement produced by the first impact of *Process and Reality*[1] (I was a member of Whitehead's classes in Harvard and Radcliffe the year that this work was published). Naturally if I were writing now I should be more cautiously critical. One is more inclined, for instance, to go in for vaguely grandiose reflections on the *Zeitgeist* at twenty-seven than at sixty. I have, however, decided to

---

[1] *Process and Reality, an Essay in Cosmology*, Gifford Lectures, Edinburgh, 1927-28 (Cambridge, 1929). See *infra*, p. 17 n.

let the book be reprinted with all its sins on its head, apart from correcting misprints and one or two obvious errors, on the grounds indicated in President Lowell of Harvard's refusal to censure undergraduate newspapers : that to change anything is to imply approval of the rest.  I do not think, however, that anything I wrote is actually misleading (if it were, it would clearly be wrong to consent to republication), though a good deal needs more critical discussion than I gave it.  I shall now try to indicate some of the main places where this is so.

In a generous review of the book in *Mind*, the late Professor Susan Stebbing drew attention very properly to the unsatisfactory discussion of what was meant by " Rationality " in Chapter III. Whitehead was continually occupied with the problem of abstraction.  How do abstract logical structures apply to concrete reality, especially if this is in part at least a fluent process ?  In *Process and Reality* he spoke with approval of Plato's having seen the problem of how one is to " seek the forms in the facts."   Following this up, I used phrases such as belief in " a logical structure in reality," a " Reason," and even " Logos " in things to which our logical schemes can correspond. I now think that it is better to confine the word " logic " to the products of our thinking, to abstract structures of propositions or symbols (verbal or non-verbal), where we can pass from premises to conclusions, and where if the premises are true the conclusions will be true. Reality as such is neither logical nor illogical, though it may of course be orderly or disorderly. The problem is the applicability of logic, so that it enables us to arrive at conclusions which will be true of reality. The most helpful discussion I know of this is Professor Popper's contribution to the symposium " Why are the Calculuses of Logic and Reality applicable to Reality? " in the Supplementary Volume xl of the *Proceedings of the Aristotelian Society*. Logical calculi have rules of inference for passing from true premises to true conclusions (Professor Ryle in a preceding paper had called these " performance rules "). When the calculi are interpreted to say something about reality, they become very general descriptive theories about certain physical facts but are not then necessarily universally true. Two apples *plus* two apples will normally make four apples (" normally," because this will not be true if the apples are left long enough to deliquesce) ; but two drops of water added to two drops of water will not make four drops of water. The question then becomes one of distinguishing properties in physical facts in virtue of which the calculus is applicable——here, that the facts are such as to contain units remaining constant over a period of time. The calculus will be applicable to the extent that the world has properties which can be formulated in terms of the calculus.

The possibility of drawing true conclusions about non-obvious aspects of the world (i.e. not simply the obvious ones such as that it contains units which can be counted) depends on elaborating more subtle forms of logic and mathematics and finding applications for them. (Whitehead could speak of mathematical forms as logical ones, since he had been engaged with Russell in *Principia Mathematica* in showing how mathematics could be derived from logic.) His views on logical-mathematical thinking affect the general character of his metaphysics[1] to a greater extent than I appreciated when I wrote this book, since, as I said in the Preface, I approached his philosophy from the background of arts and not of science and mathematics. I shall try to indicate later some of the ways in which this logico-mathematical influence is operative. Professor Victor Lowe in his book *Understanding Whitehead*[2] refers to an occasion on which John Dewey had

[1] Whitehead himself said as much in his foreword to Quine's *A System of Logistic* (Cambridge, Mass., 1934): " The reformation of Logic has an essential reference to Metaphysics. For Logic prescribes the shape of metaphysical thought."

[2] Page 276 (Johns Hopkins University, 1962). This is the most balanced all-round interpretation of Whitehead which I know.

asked Whitehead to choose between emphasis on a mathematical-formal interpretation of his philosophic method and emphasis on a genetic-functional interpretation. " Whitehead of course declined to choose, and said the real problem for philosophers was the fusion of these two ways of interpreting first principles." Whitehead was trying to hold together a way of looking on the world as made up of interconnected dynamic and fluent processes, and at the same time as exhibiting structures which could be exhibited in mathematical and logical forms. These might be invented by free speculative thinking; they might also be abstracted from perceived data by an intellectual operation of whittling out some uniformly repeated structure. Whitehead's main example of this was his Method of Extensive Abstraction, where geometrical entities such as points and lines are defined in terms of routes of approximation of overlapping sets of volumes.[1] He claimed there was an empirical basis for this, in that a volume overlapping another volume is a perceptible relation. To use this relation for defining points and lines, however, the overlap must not only be an overlap as crudely perceived, but given the exactness of a topological construction. Whitehead seems to me now to underestimate the extent to which these con-

[1] See *infra*, pp. 203 *sq.*

xvi PREFACE TO THE SECOND EDITION

structions are intellectual artefacts and to over-
estimate the extent to which they can be derived
from experienced relations. This also comes out
in his contention that the world must have a
*uniform* structure, as well as containing variable
ones, a contention both of his metaphysics and of
his philosophy of science. His reasons for this
include :

(*a*) A belief that the justification of induction
requires that experience beyond the present should
continue uniformly some at least of the characteristics found in the present.

(*b*) A belief that measurement depends on congruence, not only as the conformity between the
measuring element and what is measured, but as
an identity of function of the measuring element
when applied to different regions, this being one of
the reasons why he contends, against Einstein, for
a uniform system of space-time.

(*c*) The religious view of the importance of
" permanence," as well as change, as characteristic
of reality in at least certain of its aspects.

The first of these seems to demand relative, but
not necessarily absolute permanences. Some
characteristics of some things must remain constant over periods, if it is to be possible to make
classifications and generalizations. There may of
course be some characteristics which remain
always uniform, but I do not see that inductive

reasoning, which gives probabilities and not deductive certainties, depends on this. The second consideration, that of measurement, depends indeed on there being regular periodicities such as the movements of the heavenly bodies for measuring the passage of time, and on judgments of congruence between what is measured and calibrated scales for measuring. Changes and variations in any of these means of measurement must happen at different rates if we are to be able to detect, for example, that a clock is gaining or losing or a measuring-rod expanding. But can we say empirically that any natural events used as a scale (for example, the solar year) must always remain constant? Whitehead indeed speaks of the niform structure as being the structure of space-time. If we think of this as a completely uniform grid, is not this because we define it in this way, and not because we so discover it in natural processes? Space and Time as mathematical abstractions may be absolutely uniform (or not, according to definition). But can we say the uniformity is abstracted from events, except by making precise what is never given quite precisely? When Whitehead writes,[1] " Thus nature is a becomingness of events which are mutually significant so as to form a systematic structure. We express the character of the

[1] *The Principle of Relativity* (1922), p. 21.

2

systematic structure of events in terms of Space and Time.   Thus Space and Time are abstractions from this structure," I find the same difficulty in his notion of " abstraction " as I noted in connection with the Method of Extensive Abstraction. Empirically speaking, the question " How do we know that one hour is exactly the same length as another hour ? " seems meaningless, but it can be a truth of logic.

I am not sure how much weight to give to what Whitehead calls the religious intuition of permanence.   Certainly a good deal of religious language speaks of what is permanent and unchanging over against change, but this may be a matter of traditional ways of speaking, or of what Whitehead calls " paying metaphysical compliments to God."

None of this should be taken as an argument that there is *not* some type of unchanging and uniform, as well as changing types of order in the world.   I simply put it forward as a question as to whether Whitehead is justified in maintaining that there must be.   When I wrote this book, I accepted his statements on this too readily.

Whatever the answer to the question about a basic uniformity, that there are at least temporarily stable forms of order and repetitive regularities in the world is a fact of experience, and one on which physical science as we know it depends.

Whitehead's philosophy of nature has been a series of attempts to grapple with this fact. In the early books this was done by his distinction between " Events " and " Objects," events being slices of the temporal passage of nature, and objects being those elements such as greenness or roundness, which did not change, but recurred as characterizing events. " Objects " as such were potential characters ; as characters of actual events they were said to be " ingredient " in them. This was, of course, a way of putting in other language the old distinction of particulars and universals. It was a way of saying that the world is both a changing process and that it exhibits recognizable features, repeated either in linear stages of a slice of the process (so that we say " The tree is green ") or in different slices and regions (so that we say " Trees are green in springtime "). But to analyse this in terms of events and objects ingredient in them is not to *explain* anything ; it is simply to recommend a way of talking about what Whitehead sees as an important theoretical distinction. " Objects," though spoken of as " factors in facts," are not the kind of objects one might find, for instance on a treasure hunt. In *Process and Reality* instead of speaking of " events " and " objects," he speaks of " actual entities " and " eternal objects," and he does appear to be looking for an explanation of why there should be recognizably recurrent qualities and persisting orderly relationships within the process of nature. He lays down an Ontological Principle by which reasons for anything must be found in the composite natures of definite actual entities, not in "principles" or concepts or other such *entia rationis*. If we take this seriously, then the reason for any permanence, stability, repetition of qualities in the world, must be found in the characters of actual entities. It will not do to say "objects ingress" into them, and leave it at that. Hence Whitehead here speaks of continuities of properties and of recurrent and repeated characteristics as due to the "objectification" of actual entities in each other. There are very great difficulties in this notion—far greater than I realized when I wrote this book. I shall look at some of them presently. Here I simply raise the question of whether this way of talking does not render the notion of "eternal objects" otiose. This point was put by Everett W. Hall in an article, "Of what use are Whitehead's Eternal Objects?" in the *Journal of Philosophy,* vol. xxvii, no 20 (1930), which I now find carries conviction. He argued that the eternal objects were brought in to account for identity, permanence, universality, and potentiality. But if actual occasions are objectified in each other in linear strands, this gives the identity, for instance, of a tree over a period of time. Relative permanences can be traced to groupings of actual entities, and absolute permanence (if required) to the character of the basic actual entity, " God," whose character also makes for universal uniformities in the world and for possibilities beyond what is realised in the immediate state of the world. There are, of course, great difficulties in Whitehead's notion of God—even more than I saw when I wrote— but if we grant Whitehead's view of such an actual entity, then do we also need " eternal objects ? "

In this case, the analogies between Whitehead's later metaphysics and Platonism would be weaker than I thought when I wrote. *Process and Reality* does indeed contain a number of highly compli- mentary references to Plato ; and at the time when I was attending Whitehead's classes A. E. Taylor's *Commentary on Plato's Timaeus*[1] had just come into his possession and very much excited him. Hence the emphasis I gave this in Chapter VIII. The books that followed *Process and Reality*—*Adven- tures of Ideas*[2] and *Modes of Thought*[3]—strengthen the impression that the final outcome of his metaphysics was away from Platonism. Certainly it was a misnomer on the part of the writer of *The Times's* obituary notice to call him " the last

[1] Published in 1927.
[2] Cambridge, 1933.        [3] Cambridge, 1938.

and greatest of the Cambridge Platonists." In spite of the antitheses at the end of *Process and Reality,* his metaphysics is one of *process,* where the process displays types of order derived from the characteristics of its internally related components, including a basic component which gives it a permanent structure of a kind which allows the development of further new and changing structures.    Whatever the difficulties in this view (and they are considerable), it looks like a view of a single-world process with an immanent " ground " rather than a "two-world" view of the Platonic kind.

If we take this interpretation, rather than the more Platonic one, the notions of " objectification " and the immanence of actual entities in one another become crucial.    Here again, I find great difficulties, but there is no doubt that I underestimated the seriousness with which Whitehead maintains that actual entities, though they perish in their " subjective immediacy," not only influence but are " re-enacted " in other actual entities.    Whitehead indeed said as much in one of his rare letters, and since this might be said to be " horse's-mouth " criticism, I pass it on.

(1) " You seem to me at various points to forget my doctrine of ' immanence ' which governs the whole treatment of objectification.    Thus at times you write as tho' the connection between past and present is merely that of a transfer of

*character*.   Then there arises [*sic*] all the perplexities of ' correspondence ' in epistemology, of causality, and of memory.   The doctrine of *immanence* is fundamental.

(2) " You neglect the fundamental character of subjective form.   The subject–object relation is the emotional life of the subject derived from the objects and directed towards them.   But the drive towards self-formation is in the subjective form. The continuity in nature is a continuity of subjective form.   Cf. in the Index[1] under ' Conformal feelings ' and ' Subjective form.'   Remember that consciousness is *not* the fundamental basis of experience——so that the subject–object relation is *not* fundamentally subject–conscious–of–object.

(3) " You sometimes write as if my doctrine of sense-perception were fundamental.   For P. and R., sense perception is a highly sophisticated outcome of the higher phases of experience——and *for this reason* very prominent in consciousness—— cf. P. and R., Part IV, last chapter, also in Index under ' *Sense perception* ' or ' *Presentational Immediacy*.'

" But do not let these remarks give you the impression that I am not pleased with the book—— quite the contrary.   I have read it with profit and appreciation."

[1] Would that the index of any of Whitehead's books was adequate!

And again, writing on another occasion : " You hardly seem to emphasize my strong belief that all sentences tell us only half the truth concerning the dim consciousness of our minds.  There is always the vague feeling of things beyond us, which are also within us, and within which we live. This is the reason why we talk aloud to the world beyond and within."

So whatever the difficulties, it is clear that Whitehead's remarks about the mutual immanence of things must be considered fundamental to his view.  Probably we most of us have in our minds a dominant notion of things as affecting each other by external impact—action and reaction being in principle equal and measurable.  This in its purest form is a billiard-ball model of mutual influence.  Whitehead's own view seems to have been reached with the help of field physics and the notion of the flux of energy, which he heard expounded in lectures in Cambridge by Sir J. J. Thompson.[1]  This suggested a route of events or actual occasions as transferring energy from one to another, and so of each as receiving its energy from others.  " Energy passes from particular occasion to particular occasion.  At each point there is a flux with a quantitative flow and a

[1] *Cf. Adventures of Ideas*, p. 238. Dr. W. Mays first drew my attention to the importance of these notions in Whitehead's thought.  I had not appreciated them when I wrote.

definite direction." The properties of the quantitative flow as measured by physics abstracts from its inner quality as entertained by the particular actual occasion—its " subjective form." When both aspects are taken into account, Whitehead says, " the energetic activity considered in physics is the emotional intensity entertained in life."[1] That energy experienced from within is emotionally toned is certainly a hard doctrine, especially when we go below the level of living organisms, and, as a generalization, it is hard enough even there. It is not made easier by Whitehead's extending the terminology of emotion, especially the term " feeling," to cover relations formerly discussed under the term " prehensions." True, he tells us[2] that " feeling " is a mere technical term " chosen to suggest that functioning through which the concrescent actuality appropriates the datum so as to make it its own," and insists that it must be dissociated from the special and rare condition of being conscious. But if a technical term is needed, perhaps his former term " prehension " is less disturbing than the use of the ordinary language term " feeling " in so Pickwickian a sense. Be this as it may, it is evident that Whitehead holds that subjective forms as ways of feeling are not just private to the subject

[1] *Modes of Thought*, p. 232.
[2] *Process and Reality*, p. 229 (249).

2*

that feels (the private aspect he calls " subjective immediacy "), and that they are transferred to other actual occasions, which reproduce them, not necessarily just as they were, but modified by their own subjective forms.   In this way, he says, the character of one thing does not just conform to that of another, but inherits its actual " feelings " and incorporates them in its own constitution.   This is the " objective immortality " of past in present occasions.

I must admit that I find this view of the immanence of one thing in others through the re-enactment of " feelings " extremely difficult, and I do not know that anyone has really elucidated it.   Professor Christian had a try in his *An Interpretation of Whitehead's Metaphysics* [1] but came down on the view that what are repeated from one actual occasion to another are characteristics. This is undoubtedly the view which is easiest to make plausible, and I was inclined to it myself ; but we have Whitehead's emphatic statement that it is not what he meant.   Possibly part of what could be meant by these qualitative conservations might be put some day in terms of Communications Theory. [2]   This is concerned not just with

[1]  Yale, 1959.

[2]  That there might be some connection between Whitehead's later metaphysics and Communications Theory was first suggested to me by a remark of Margaret Masterman.   She is, however,

the Conservation of Energy, but with the canalizing of structures which enable information to be transferred from one stage in a process to another —hence the attractive phrase " negative entropy " has been used of Information.    But even if the conservation of Information might be relevant to part of what Whitehead is saying, could this be held to include conservation of emotional tone? (I tried to elucidate what this might mean in connection with Whitehead's theory of Perception in the Mode of Causal Efficacy in my *The Nature of Metaphysical Thinking*,[1] where I criticized the view that sensa such as a perception of green, projected on the world of "presentational immediacy", could really plausibly be said to be derived from a feeling characterising our own bodily states.    Those who find the discussion of sense-perception in the present book too short and insufficiently critical may perhaps care to refer to this fuller treatment.)

Whitehead insists that sense-perception is a rare and special case of a general activity of the " prehension " of some entities by others.    This is an instance of a difficulty I find throughout his notion of " descriptive generalization."    Is it

---

not responsible for my suggesting that there might be an interpretation of the notion of Objective Immortality along these lines.

[1] Pp. 44-48, and Appendix, pp. 228-234.

xxviii PREFACE TO THE SECOND EDITION

right to assume that the same categories must apply to everything that exists, and to every kind of activity, or may there be genuine differences in the principles by which some of these should be described? Whitehead takes the former line; he adopts categories mainly appropriate to psycho-physiological activities (e.g. " feelings "), and stretches these upwards and downwards. When stretched upwards, this means he minimizes the difference that is made where consciousness and intelligence is present; downwards, it means that something like subjective emotional experience gets attributed to what we should normally call non-living matter. Also his method of generali-zation leads to his speaking of things which may belong to different levels of abstraction—for instance fundamental particles, biological orga-isms, human societies—as though they were all systems of actual entities in a similar sense and so could interact with each other. Even allowing a realist, not a phenomenalist, view of fundamental particles, surely a good deal more theoretical construction goes into the view of what they may be than goes into accounts of biological organisms.

In consequence of his view of the " immanence" of things in one another, Whitehead has seemed committed to a view of universal internal relations, so as to run into the difficulties of the Idealist philosophers, of having to say that everything in the universe modifies everything else, and that nothing can change without changing everything else. I have mentioned some of the ways in which he seeks to avoid this extreme view.[1] Lest these may seem somewhat verbal ways of avoiding it, I want to call attention to one crucial limitation on universal mutual conditioning which I failed to note. This is the causal independence of *contemporary* actual occasions. The Absolute Idealist's world of internally related elements was a "block universe." Whitehead's world is a pluralistic process with many strands of actual occasions "in unison of becoming." Each arises out of its prehensions of the world of its immediate past (and on any view it is surely hard to say how far environmental influences may extend). But its immediate present existence, which includes its "subjective aim" as a spearhead of development, is contemporaneous and so causally independent of a whole gamut of other similar actual occasions (since contemporary events cannot interact). Whitehead also allows some capacity for original response in the actual entity in its immediacy. So we are not caught in a net of universal mutual conditioning with no room for manœuvre, no freedom, no novelty.

Whitehead's view of actual entities as inter-

[1] See *infra*, pp. 129-131.

related in " societies " and " societies of societies,"
and as transmitting dominant social characteristics,
has had its echoes in work by various people who
have been writing about Sociology in and out of
Harvard during the last thirty years. I think
that applications can be made here, especially
since the notion of internal relations is one which
seems congenial to sociologists, with their interest
in mutually conditioning factors within systems
of relationships. They also need to think about
limitations on conformity to mutual conditioning,
and the possibility of there being a measure of
original response on the part of individuals.

Difficulties over the notion of mutual immanence
come to a head in Whitehead's view of the " Consequent Nature of God." The notion of the
" Primordial Nature of God " is hard enough.
It seems, as a basic order limiting pure Creativity,
to be a kind of cosmic propositional function—
the form of an indefinite number of actual propositions, when values are supplied to its variables.
It is not, however, only this; or, as Dr. Mays
suggested, the structure of extensive connection
as the most general kind of order underlying more
specific kinds of order. Whitehead continually
insists that the Primordial Nature of God must
also consist in " appetition", a drive towards the
realization in actual occasions of the values made
possible by this basic order. Is there an am-

biguity here in " values ", which covers both the
ethically and aesthetically neutral logical notion of
supplying values to variables, and the teleological
notion of value as something which for some
reason it is good to achieve? Whitehead's notion
of the Primordial Nature of God as including
" an aim at value " seems to cover both these
senses. It seems to be a " ground of being "
view ; one for which there is a basic structure-cum-
drive in everything that exists. Beyond this, the
" Consequent Nature of God " seems, put very
crudely, to be the reaction of God's " appetition "
to what actual entities of the world process are
making out of the initial subjective aims and
possibilities for realization afforded them by the
Primordial Nature of God. Since Whitehead
says that God is an actual entity to whom the same
categories apply as to all other actual entities, he
will be a " concrescence of prehensions," a
unification of all the other actual entities into a new
unity. I used the expression " the measure of
harmony " achieved in the process of the world
at any stage ; this was a vague and unsatisfactory
way of putting this notion of a particular unification
from the particular point of view of a divine
Monad. But Whitehead's actual entities, unlike
Leibniz's Monads, are not windowless ; their
" perceptions " are prehensions which involve the
" objectification " of the data perceived in their

own developing natures. (I have said that Whitehead insists on this, however difficult it is to see just what it means.) So God's prehension of the other actual entities means their " objectification " in his own developing " Consequent " Nature (modified, no doubt, by his subjective aim). Hence Whitehead says that while actual entities perish subjectively, they are " objectively immortal " in the Consequent Nature of God. There is a problem here that I had not noted when I wrote. Since only actual entities in the *past* can be objectified in a present developing actual entity, actual entities which perish could be objectified in the Consequent Nature of God. But there cannot be " mutual immanence " of the Consequent Nature of God in other actual entities, since this is an actual entity which has not yet become, and so cannot be in the past of other entities. When does it become, and achieve " satisfaction ? " Never, as far as I can see, if it is " everlasting " and " with all creation," since there is no evidence that Whitehead thinks of a terminal point of the process, a " far off divine event to which the whole creation moves." There seem to be two possible interpretations. Either God in his combined Primordial and Consequent Natures is *an* actual entity, but unlike others " everlasting "; in his Consequent Nature he continually objectifies all other actual entities, but since he never becomes and perishes, he cannot be objectified in them. Or God might be thought of, not as an actual entity, but as a "route" of actual entities, such as "enduring objects" like rocks, trees, and our own persons are said to be, each supervening on and objectifying its predecessor into its own make-up, inheriting not only from its predecessors along the route, but from the other actual entities of its world. The latter interpretation would allow for the objectification of the actual entities comprising the route into others of the environing world, as well as their objectification in it, and would bring the notion of God closer to the notion of other actual entities in Whitehead's scheme. It would, however, mean saying that God is not *an actual entity,* but a "route" of actual entities, and Whitehead certainly does say that he is an actual entity. I think that the first interpretation is closer to what Whitehead says, but I question whether he has seen the difficulty in the notion of an "everlasting" actual entity. This breaks his rule that the same categories should apply to all actual entities, since these are defined as perpetually perishing, and when perished subjectively able to be in each other's pasts, while contemporaneous actual entities are causally independent. Hence an actual entity whose process of concrescence is contemporaneous with the whole world cannot be objectified in it.    What Whitehead says about the immanence of God in the world would therefore have to apply not to the Consequent, but the Primordial Nature of God, as a basic order-cum-drive in things.

This is an instance of the difficulty which besets other attempts at natural theology as well as Whitehead's.    Things are said about God which would only make sense if he were one actual entity (or " *a* being ") among others, only greater and grander, and at the same time other things are said which, if pressed, show that he cannot be this.

I admit, however, that I can now only approach Whitehead's natural theology with considerable hesitancy, both as to what it means, and as to whether it is really integral to a view of the world as made up of a pluralism of concrescent processes, whose " laws of nature " are defined by the dominant structures displayed in their interrelations. There is the question of whether there must be some basic structure, and whether this must be thought of as uniform, permanent, and still more, as including not only structure but " appetition " towards the realization of the " values " (in both senses) which it makes possible, and whether there is any reason to think of this realization as " good."    Those who want to pursue further the lines of thought suggested by Whitehead's natural theology can, I believe, best do so by reading the

works of Professor Hartshorne.[1]    This is particularly so because Professor Hartshorne tells us
that he had arrived at his main convictions about
the natural theology of a " bipolar" God in which
the aspect of process is essential before he met
Whitehead's metaphysics, and that he was re-
inforced in developing his own views through
reflecting on Whitehead's.

As regards other interpreters, I find Professor
Victor Lowe's attempts[2] come nearest to grasping
the many-sidedness of Whitehead's thought.    He
has lived with it long and lovingly, and yet is by
no means an uncritical commentator.    Dr. Ivor
Leclerc[3] links Whitehead's metaphysics with
traditional Aristotelian problems and discussions,
and does this with considerable learning, but he
does not take into account the philosophy of
science.    Nathaniel Lawrence[4] does this for the
earlier books, but stops at *Process and Reality*,
when the chickens begin to come home to roost.
Dr. Mays[5] has seen the importance of certain

[1] See especially *The Logic of Perfection* (Open Court Publish-
ing House, 1962), and his contribution ' Whitehead's Idea of
God," in vol. iii of *The Library of Living Philosophers*.

[2] Especially his *Understanding Whitehead* (Johns Hopkins
University, 1961).

[3] *Whitehead's Metaphysics* (London, 1958).

[4] *Whitehead's Philosophical Development*. University of
California, 1956.

[5] *The Philosophy of Whitehead* (London, 1959).    I consider
Mays' " The relevance of ' On Mathematical Concepts of the

scientific notions, especially those of field physics, and of the continuing influence of the early work in Symbolic Logic. But his interpretation of Whitehead, though helpful in bringing out these influences, is over-simplified by not taking account of the aesthetic, religious and literary interests. These complicate the interpretation of Whitehead, though they also give him more depth.

I hope, however, that the days of books of comment and exposition (including this one) will soon be over.[1] If Whitehead is to enjoy "objective immortality" in philosophy, it will be through the stimulus of some of his seminal ideas in the independent work of other people. Margaret Masterman has suggested that a future for some of his later thought may lie in the finding of analogues developed with mathematical techniques over limited fields, and she instances a way of considering fundamental quantal particles as analogues to prehensions, and studies of the foundations of symbolism—that is of language. Other possibilities might be in work on the borders

---

Material World ' to Whitehead's Philosophy," in *The Relevance of Whitehead* (ed. I. Leclerc, London, 1961), the most valuable contribution he has made to interpretation of Whitehead.

[1] A discussion and list of these in languages other than English has been contributed by George L. Kline in *Process and Divinity* (Essays presented to Charles Hartshorne, ed. by W. L. Reese and E. Freeman. Open Court, 1964).

between the physical and biological sciences; the problems of continuity and discontinuity of structures within wider structures in dynamic processes, as in general system theories, and perhaps in sociology. If any of Whitehead's thought has a bearing on such questions, it will no doubt be developed in a different terminology, and in ways which he might not have foreseen, but might nevertheless have welcomed.

THE UNIVERSITY, MANCHESTER,
*September*, 1965.

DOROTHY EMMET

# PREFACE TO THE FIRST EDITION

THERE is no substitute for the first-hand study of a philosopher; and if this book were to be looked on as in any way intended as a summary or epitome of Professor Whitehead's Philosophy of Organism, it had better never have been written. It represents simply an attempt on the part of one of his students to acknowledge something of her debt to his work and his wisdom; and to discuss some of the ideas in it which have seemed to her of special significance.

My first reason for daring to venture on this is simply my interest in and affection for Professor Whitehead and his writings. My second is the growing suspicion that there are a number of people of philosophical interests who are asking for an introduction to the study of his metaphysics, especially of *Process and Reality*. If this book should send any back with renewed encouragement to re-reading Professor Whitehead's own later books, that is the best outcome I should hope for from it.

And here, at the outset, I must make an apology and an explanation. Throughout the greater part of his life, Professor Whitehead's own work has been in pure mathematics; and although his later books have contained practically no technical mathematical reasoning, or even mathematical logic, I am continually conscious that the way in which his mind is working is essentially that of a pure mathematician. I have the uneasy suspicion that however much notions like that of Extensive Connection and the Method of Extensive Abstraction may seem clear, they probably connote something quite different to someone with a trained understanding of the mathematical ideas involved in them. My own knowledge of the mathematical side of Professor Whitehead's work is confined to a none too confident acquaintance with the philosophical sections at the beginning of the *Principia Mathematica*, and to his *Introduction to Mathematics* (H.U.L.). From these, and from Russell's books, I think I have been able to grasp something of the general ideas which form the foundations of modern mathematics, as far as to be able to distinguish between those parts of Professor Whitehead's work which call for a more specialised mathematical knowledge on the part of the reader, and those which can be comprehensible to the ordinary person of philosophical interests, and a general idea, but no very detailed knowledge, of the foundations of mathematics. Such I take to be the situation in which a great many of us who wish to learn from Professor Whitehead find ourselves; and it is as such and for such that I have written.   I claim no more than to be trying to show how Professor Whitehead's philosophical work strikes a student who comes to it from a background of literary instead of scientific philosophy.   If the experiment fails, and it is not for us to understand it, I can only accept the rebuke.

But I have a suspicion that Professor Whitehead himself does not think of the ideas contained in what he calls his Philosophy of Organism as only to be available to a closed circle of mathematicians and logicians.   Moreover, the opinions of some of these about his Gifford Lectures seem to suggest that they think that his mathematical genius is losing itself in a welter of pseudo-Platonic mysticism.   It may be, therefore, that there are sides of this later work whose defence can fall to some of us whose interests in philosophy are necessarily humanist rather than mathematical.   I am not saying anything against the mathematicians and mathematical logicians— I envy them too deeply for that.   But the adventure of rationalism is a many-sided one, and happily its pursuit must be co-operative.

I wish to thank the Commonwealth Fund of New York and the Council of Somerville College for electing me to research fellowships which have made it possible to undertake this work. My greatest personal obligation is to Professor Whitehead himself, for his inspiration and encouragement. He very kindly read some papers which now form part of the present work, and I have gone forward with it with his permission. Needless to say, I alone am responsible for any misunderstandings of his theories which it may contain. Canon Raven and my former teachers, the Master of Balliol and Mr. C. R. Morris, have read through the whole book in MS., and made valuable suggestions. My gratitude to them for this is but a small part of what I owe their constant friendship.

D. M. E.

OXFORD,
*September*, 1931.

# CHAPTER I

## INTRODUCTORY

This picklock Reason is still a-fumbling at the wards,
bragging to unlock the door of stern Reality.

*The Testament of Beauty.*

A REVIEWER of Whitehead's Gifford Lectures,
*Process and Reality*,[1] states the dilemma in which
a good many of us must have felt ourselves after
reading them. Either, she says, the thought
is too profound to be judged by our generation,
or they are the product of thought which is essentially unclear, but illuminated throughout by
flashes of penetrating insight.

If the former alternative be right, all we can hope
to do is to follow as far as we can, and leave the
understanding of the rest to the philosophical dis-
cernment of our descendants. If the latter, we can
at least try to discover the jewels in the mass of
surrounding clay, and meditate on these " flashes
of penetrating insight," which even the most
unsympathetic critic must acknowledge are to
be found in Whitehead's work. The former
alternative may be right; but it is not a judgment
that a mere student of philosophy such as the

---

[1] Miss Stebbing, in *Mind*, October, 1930.

present writer is competent to make. There
may be a temptation to many to accept the latter
alternative. For no present-day philosopher is
more quoted than Whitehead, and better known
by his aphorisms; whereas the relation of his
aphorisms to the body of his thought is not always
apparent to those who quote him.

This book, however, is not committed to accepting either of these opinions as a final verdict. I
shall try to maintain that there is a very real connection between the general ideas of Whitehead's
system and the "flashes of insight"; that the
meaning of the latter is only to be properly dis-
cerned, without interpreting them in a way which
he himself would neither mean nor wish, in terms
of the former; and, on the other hand, that if
these "flashes of insight," which we say illuminate
and make significant some part of our experience,
can be shown to be important applications of
the general ideas of the system, it adds considerable weight to those ideas.

A proper grasp of the context of a philosophical
idea in the system of a philosopher is essential to
the understanding of its significance. This seems
an elementary truism, but it is surprising to see
how often it is neglected, especially by those
who like to quote, perhaps, the religious opinions
of a philosopher, and interpret or criticise them
in the terms and associations of another system

of ideas. This is particularly disastrous in dealing with the ideas of a philosopher like Whitehead; and we shall see the reason when we come to discuss his particular view of philosophic method and the nature of systematic speculative philosophy. There is a sense, no doubt, in which general ideas can be distinguished from the parochialism (to use a word of Whitehead's own) of their time and setting; and if the history of philosophy is to be more than a history of philosophers and their peculiar opinions, it should be a tracing of the way in which the universal aspects of ideas become gradually clarified and distinguished from the mythology and particularities of the system of thought in which they were born. But in trying to do this without an initial understanding of the systems of thought we are on dangerous ground. There is also a sense in which the system and the penetrating idea stand together, even if, fortunately, it need not always be true that they must stand and fall together.

This claim (which I shall seek to defend in the next two chapters) that the business of metaphysics is to create penetrating general ideas which may make some part of our experience more significant, may be read as a protest against the prevalent fashion of making an absolute division of the problems of philosophy into those which may

be solved with practical certainty by mathematical logic, and those which cannot, and which
are therefore said to be insoluble, and must be
left to " mystical feeling."[1]

This all or nothing view of the function of
logic, if taken seriously, would do away entirely
with the value of philosophy, as it has proved itself
over and over again, in the gradual clarifying and
making more significant of any elements whatever
in the welter of experience upon which we like
to philosophise.   While agreeing with Wittgenstein,[2] and the school of logicians he represents,
that the object of philosophy is essentially eluci-
datory, the logical clarification of ideas, I should
part company with him when he says that this
implies that it should limit the thinkable and the
unthinkable.[3]   I shall urge that Whitehead is
right in saying that there is no such hard-and-fast
distinction—no problems which as such do not
admit of philosophical treatment.   When there-

[1] See chapter vi., " On Scientific Method in Philosophy,"
in Russell's *Mysticism and Logic* (London, 1918), especially
pp. 110 *sq.*; and such, I take it, is the outcome of Wittgenstein's
view of philosophy as an activity and not a subject, reducible
in the end to " important nonsense."

[2] *Tractatus Logico-Philosophicus* (London, 1922), 4. 112.

[3] 4. 114.   We may contrast Whitehead's remark, *Science
and the Modern World* (Cambridge, 1926), p. 258 : " In an
intellectual age there can be no active interest which puts aside
all hope of a vision of the harmony of truth."

fore he leaves the comparative clarity and distinctness of symbolic logic and natural knowledge for the more elusive and vaguer problems of existence and value, he may not succeed in solving them satisfactorily, but at least he has a right to make the attempt; and any of us who have the will and obligation to be rational, if only from " the sentiment of rationality," may make an attempt to follow him. We may also hope that a mind like his, trained in the appreciation of rationality, will be able to help us to discover some order amid the confusion, instead of blaming him too quickly for attempting to systematise and rationalise the " irrational."

In an informal speech at the Seventh International Congress of Philosophy, Whitehead suggested that the spirit of modern philosophy, and the stage which its speculations have reached, is almost exactly that of the Pre-Socratics. Perhaps one way in which this may be seen is that, like the Ionian cosmologists, we are coming to look on these human problems of value and conduct as far harder than the problems of " natural knowledge." When, therefore, a natural philosopher like Whitehead comes to treat them, with a full understanding of the difficulties involved, and a knowledge of what clear thinking means in the mathematical sciences, we must not expect the results to be easily understood.

The fault lies not only with the natural philosopher, but with the subject-matter. At any rate we can come confidently to one opinion—that the nature of things is not simple, but of a baffling complexity. We sometimes hear, for instance from a reviewer complaining of his failure to understand *Process and Reality*, that these things have been hid from the wise and prudent and revealed to babes. There may be, and surely is, a sense in which this can be so, but as a judgment on the value of a philosophical work, it too often simply hides mental laziness. There is, as William James says, a thick and a thin simplicity. The thick simplicity can only be achieved by those who appreciate the complexity and difficulties of the subject-matter, and yet also see that there can, nevertheless, be a certain, perhaps we may say, moral simplicity in our attitude in trying to understand it. This we might describe as an attitude of open-minded reasonableness, combined with an attempt to arrive at the greatest possible economy and clarity of concepts in our attempted explanations. So, as Whitehead himself puts it,[1] the guiding motto in the life of every natural philosopher should be "seek simplicity and distrust it."

The task of anyone who would set out to be a speculative metaphysician in these days is

[1] *Concept of Nature* (Cambridge, 1920), p. 163.

certainly stupendous enough. In fact, with a view to our increasing appreciation of the complexity of the subject-matter with which he has to deal, it is demanded of the modern metaphysician that he be a kind of superman. He must have a wide knowledge of philosophy, logic, pure mathematics, and, it would seem, of the philosophical side of scientific thought, especially of physics, besides the constructive genius to be able to create some sort of picture of what seems to be the outcome of it all. And this at a time when knowledge has become more and more highly specialised, so that only the specialist understands his own field, and no one can, like Aristotle or St. Thomas Aquinas, claim a comprehensive knowledge of the whole volume of contemporary ideas, and set them out in a system which claims to answer all the questions which a reasonable man could possibly be expected to ask. So it is not surprising to find few who still believe in the possibility of constructing comprehensive philosophical systems, and many even who think that the day of old-fashioned speculative metaphysics has gone by. Others may say that the concepts of modern philosophical and scientific thought are still so tentative and provisional that the time has not yet come for anyone to try to synthesise them in a metaphysical scheme.

3

It therefore means a real break with the spirit of most modern philosophy for Whitehead to claim that it is the business of the philosopher to try to formulate a synoptic metaphysical system. We feel in reading him that in this way he is much closer to the Greeks and Cartesians, perhaps above all to Leibniz, than to most modern philosophers (with the obvious exception of Professor Alexander), and certainly than to most of those of the recent past.

I shall try to point out some reasons for this in the next two chapters, in considering his view of philosophic method, and his defence of rationalist speculative philosophy, and shall ask how far we can hold that his attempt is legitimate. The rest of the book will begin to explore how far it is successful.

# CHAPTER II

In the immense majority of men, even in civilized countries, speculative philosophy has ever been, and must remain, a *terra incognita*, yet all the epoch-making revolutions of the Christian world, the revolutions of religion, and with them the civil, social and domestic habits of the nations concerned, have coincided with the rise and fall of metaphysical systems.—COLERIDGE.

Nothing can be conceived more hard than the heart of a thoroughbred metaphysician. It comes nearer to the cold malignity of a wicked spirit than to the frailty and passion of a man. It is like that of the principle of evil himself, incorporeal, pure, unmixed, dephlegmated, defecated evil.—BURKE.

What is it that I employ my metaphysics on ? To perplex our clearest notions and living moral instincts ? To extinguish the light of love and of conscience, to put out the life of arbitrament, to make myself and others worthless, soulless, Godless ? No, to expose the folly and legerdemain of those who have thus abused the blessed organ of language, to support all old and venerable truths, to support, to kindle, to project, to make the reason spread light over our feelings, to make our feelings diffuse vital warmth through our reason—these are my objects, and these my subjects. Is this the metaphysic that bad spirits in hell delight in ?—COLERIDGE.

THE preface to *Process and Reality* states White-head's view of the scope and aim of his work. Since these statements would by no means be generally accepted—in fact, as I have said, they run directly counter to the spirit of most modern philosophy—it may be worth while to quote them in full and to spend some time in discussing them.

(a) " That the movement of historical and philosophical criticism of detached questions, which on the whole has dominated the last two centuries, has done its work, and requires to be supplemented by a more sustained effort of constructive thought.

(b) " That the true method of philosophical construction is to frame a scheme of ideas, the best that one can, and unflinchingly to explore the interpretation of experience in terms of that scheme.

(c) " All constructive thought . . . is dominated by some such scheme, unacknowledged but no less influential in guiding the imagination. The importance of philosophy lies in its sustained effort to make such schemes explicit, and thereby capable of criticism and improvement.

(d) " The final reflection—how shallow, puny and imperfect are efforts to sound the depths in the nature of things. In philosophical discussion the merest hint of dogmatic certainty as to finality of statement is an exhibition of folly."

In this chapter I wish to consider what Whitehead means by a Speculative Philosophy, in the broadest sense, in the light of these four reflections. In the next chapter I shall go on to ask whether he has sufficiently taken account of the various objections which can be raised against this type of philosophy.

" Speculative Philosophy " is defined[1] as " the endeavour to frame a coherent, logical and necessary system of general ideas in terms of which every element of our experience can be interpreted." This sounds an ambitious enough task; but before questioning its possibility, we must see how he describes it in the succeeding paragraphs of *Process and Reality*, and, more particularly, in *The Function of Reason*.[2]

In this book he has given us a vigorous defence of a rationalistic method in Science and Philosophy. He introduces this by a definition and description of what he means by Reason, and the part it has played in evolution and civilization. His definition of Reason (which we must accept provisionally) is " the self-discipline of the originative element in life," that is to say, the ordering of an urge towards novelty which, as we shall see, he says is a " mental pole," possessed in some measure by every actuality. The primary

[1] *Process and Reality*, Pt. I., ch. i., § 1.

[2] *The Function of Reason* (Princeton, 1929). This is quite the most straightforward, and in many ways the most suggestive and delightful of Whitehead's books (*cf.* the review in *Mind*, October, 1930).

function of Reason, in this sense, is simply the promotion of life. This is the function of what he calls the Practical Reason, understanding this in the pragmatic sense, namely as an instrument for discovering means to ends imaginatively grasped as desirable. This is not necessarily, and in fact comparatively rarely, conscious—it is an originative urge towards a different situation. He gives as an example the urge to find means to satisfy thirst in the desert, where the natural physical tendency is simply towards drought, while the counter-tendency is an activity to find a means to maintain life. This counter-tendency, like Bergson's *élan vital*, we may call a feeling after a means to fuller life. In its higher phases it becomes conscious, instrumental intelligence.[1] He connects Reason in this sense with the story of Odysseus—Reason symbolised by the cunning of the foxes.[2]

But there is the other side of Reason which he connects with the name of Plato—Reason shared not with the foxes, but with the gods—Reason as seeking not an immediate method of action, but some understanding of things.[3] The history of Reason in this sense is very short—

[1] *Op. cit.*, pp. 29-32 ; 7.

[2] This view of the Practical Reason will be further discussed when we come to the notion of " mental prehensions." It can only be noticed here in passing.       [3] *Ibid.*, pp. 31-32.

it belongs only to the 6,000 years, perhaps, of civilization. Whitehead ascribes the discovery of its supreme importance to the Greeks. Its general characteristic is its power of transcending any immediate and obvious practical aim, and so of gaining some synoptic vision of things. Its aim is some wider generalisation; that is to say, the discovery of some connection in things which will be significant beyond the particularity of the immediate instance. Since it is free from any direct relevance to a practical end, it can try to reach these wider generalisations by the free play of imagination. But the free play of imagination alone, springing from religious and artistic inspiration, is like prophecy; it is wild, anarchic, and, though it contains perhaps important truths, it is without the means of discipline and self-criticism. (We may recall Plato's discussion of μανία in the *Phaedrus*.) So Whitehead has some hard sayings about prophets,[1] suggesting, with quiet irony, that without some method of testing, it is perhaps best to stone them in some merciful way. This is perhaps natural for one who realises as clearly as he does, the importance and the precariousness of rationality in what we call our civilized life; and how easy it is for the natural man—who, as he says, emending Aristotle, is after all but " an animal intermit-

[1] *Op. cit.*, p. 52.

tently liable to rationality "—to slip back into
force and fanaticism, and destroy the subtler and
more delicate orders built upon Reason.    Yet he
would surely be among the first to agree

> That 'tis a thing impossible to frame
> Conceptions equal to the soul's desire :
> And the most difficult of tasks to keep
> Heights which the soul is competent to gain.

It is the paradox that without disciplined Reason,
no heights can be kept for long; yet, anti-intellec-
tualist and even vandal though the prophet often
is, without him there might be no heights gained.
Moreover, Whitehead sees in the sporadic inspira-
tions of prophecy the germ of the Speculative
Reason—the imaginative grasp at a possibility
which transcends existing ways of thought.

The importance of the Greeks in the history of
thought lies in the fact that they discovered that
the Speculative Reason itself could be subjected
to order—Logic, in the broadest sense, is the
self-discipline of speculative thought.[1]    Whitehead here seems to suggest that the Greek formal
logic was the perfect instrument for this; but no
doubt all he can mean is that it laid down
the general lines on which the self-discipline
of imaginative thought could proceed.    This is
through bringing its speculations into conformity

[1] *Op. cit.*, p. 53.

with the conditions of rational coherence.   Since these conditions are relevant not only to beliefs, but to schemes for developing them, we may pause here and spend some time in examining them.   They are defined as:

(i.) Conformity to intuitive experience.
(ii.) Clarity of the propositional content.
(iii.) Internal logical consistency.
(iv.) External logical consistency.
(v.) Status of a *Logical* scheme with,
    (*a*) widespread conformity to experience,
    (*b*) no discordance with experience,
    (*c*) coherence among its categorical notions,
    (*d*) methodological consequences.

It is a little difficult to grasp what he means by these conditions, and they do not seem to be altogether mutually independent.   The first should mean that there is something fatally wrong with philosophical ideas if they fail to find a place for what we cannot possibly doubt.   An example would be Hume's denial of any continuity in the self, or any intimate connection between the self of the present sensation with the self of the immediate past—let us say of half a second ago.   If our theory is to be in conformity with intuitive experience we should be able to give a reason at

3*

any rate for our *feeling* of derivation from our immediate past (even if it is only to show why we are under a persistent illusion). Perhaps we may say that it is failure to satisfy this criterion which marks all those theories which C. D. Broad has described as " silly " theories; which does not mean that they are not very often highly ingenious, but that they are theories which we cannot possibly hold (any more than could Hume) when we are not actually philosophising. Broad quotes Solipsism as an example of this kind of theory; and I should be inclined to add the suggestion of some of our philosophical scientists that we are all nothing but statistical probabilities.[1]

But it is a mistake to think that this criterion, or any of the others, is an easy one to apply. Intuitive experience there may be; but in saying whether any philosophical proposition is in conformity with it, we have to pass from intuition to the dubiousness and uncertainty of its statement and interpretation. " Accordingly our attitude towards an immediate intuition must be that of the gladiators, ' Morituri te salutamus,' as we pass

[1] There is, of course, another way of putting the view here alluded to which makes it much more plausible, and probably right; namely, to say that the happening of anything anywhere and at any time is a statistical probability. But when it does happen, it is surely just then that it is *not* a probability, but a " stubborn fact," however difficult, and perhaps impossible it is to say what a " fact " may be.

into the limbo where we rely upon the uncertain record."[1]

The second criterion—clarity of propositional content—is easy to accept as an ideal, but extremely hard to attain. Perhaps part of the chief value of modern logic lies in its recognising so frankly that part of the essential business of philosophy is to clarify our ideas and to arrive at symbolisms which will enable us to state them unambiguously. The result may at first seem thin and pedestrian, but unless we value the vagueness and mythology of most of our language above definiteness and precision, we must own that modern logic is doing something very important, in so far as philosophy is "an unusually determined attempt to think clearly " and to say what we mean.

Thirdly, there must be internal logical consistency. This is not simply the readily acceptable intellectual ideal of coherence; that is to say, of the mutual implication of principles which are nevertheless independent in the sense that no one of them simply overlaps or repeats another. It is also stated as a criterion of the truth of individual

[1] *Process and Reality*, p. 379 (409). (References to *Process and Reality* throughout will quote the page numbers of both the Cambridge University Press edition [1929], and of Macmillan's edition [New York, 1929], the latter reference being inserted in brackets.)

propositions, that they must not be self-contradictory.    There are some good remarks on coherence as a relation between different proposition in *Process and Reality* ch. i., § 2.    We are told that the requirement of coherence is " the great preservative of rationalistic sanity "; that is to say, it judges the relevance of ideas grasped in moments of imaginative insight, which, apart from this discipline, would be simply wild and sporadic. Incoherence, on the other hand, is " the arbitrary disconnection of first principles."    For example, we have Descartes's two kinds of substance.    It may seem obvious to a common-sense view that there are minds, and there are bodies ; but there is no sufficient reason in the Cartesian system why there should be two kinds of substance rather than one.    A rational scheme, on the other hand, must at least be coherent.    If it is to be adequate to experience, and not merely a system of possible forms of relatedness, it may have to satisfy other requirements beyond this, but coherent at least it must be.    For " Faith in reason is the trust that the ultimate natures of things lie together in a harmony which excludes mere arbitrariness.    It is the faith that at the base of things we shall not find mere arbitrary mystery."[1]

It is more difficult to see what is meant by the fourth criterion, of external logical consistency.

[1] *Science and the Modern World*, p. 26.

It is probably meant to be supplementary to the third; that is to say, while the latter demands freedom from internal contradiction in a given proposition, the former demands coherence with further propositions also accepted as true in various fields of experience.    We are indeed explicitly told[1] that it means the comparison of " the proposition under scrutiny with other propositions accepted as true."    This, as it stands, suggests that when we come to *metaphysical* propositions we should compare propositions which form part of a metaphysical scheme, with propositions derived from other sources, and that they should be consistent.    But if the metaphysical scheme is adequate and comprehensive it would be a matrix from which true propositions could be derived applying in a variety of fields.    If these clash with the propositions in fact used in these fields and accepted as true, this would be external inconsistency.    If, on the other hand, " external logical consistency " means consistency with the data of experience, it is difficult to see wherein it differs from " conformity to intuitive experience."    It would seem therefore that this condition should be understood in the sense I have suggested; though it must be admitted that it is open to the interpretation that the propositions of one scheme of thought should be judged by their

[1] *The Function of Reason*, p. 54.

consistency with the propositions of other schemes of thought, which would be counter to what has been said[1] as to the proper understanding of an idea in its context. Analogies drawn between the ideas of one scheme and those of another may indeed add more weight to the ideas; but they are only a test of truth if they are asserting or denying something in the same sense.

The fifth criterion is rather different in kind from the others, and applies to logical schemes, not to individual propositions. It suggests a way in which a logical scheme can be partially and progressively verified, when there can be no decisive testing by means of the first four criteria. It is evidently " a procedure to remedy the difficulty of judging individual propositions, by having recourse to a system of ideas, whose mutual relevance shall lend to each other clarity, and which hang together so that the verification of some reflects upon the verification of the others. Also if the system has the character of suggesting methodologies of which it is explanatory, it gains the character of generating ideas coherent with itself and receiving continuous verification."[2] By a methodology is meant a practical way of approach, or method of procedure, in the solu-

---

[1] *Cf.* supra, p. 2.
[2] *Function of Reason,* p. 55.

tion of problems. That a scheme of ideas should issue in practical applications is an important result (even if it is not, as the pragmatists would say, the only test, and whole meaning)[1] of its truth, since it is a measure of its contact with observed fact.

But although important advances in civilization have been made when the Speculative and the methodological, or Practical, Reason have come together, Whitehead is never tired of pointing out the inestimable value in the history of thought of systems of abstract ideas, undertaken primarily simply as flights of imaginative speculation, and long afterwards found to have important, and perhaps quite unforeseen, practical applications. As a mathematician he can here speak with direct knowledge, because one of the most outstanding verifications of this principle is the way in which the progress of science and technology

---

[1] For one difficulty of the pragmatic test is to decide how long a run we are to give a proposition before saying whether or not it works.  So, as Whitehead says (*Process and Reality*, p. 256 [275]), " the poor pragmatist remains an intellectual Hamlet, perpetually adjourning decision of judgment to some later date."  Tocqueville summed up a discussion with a friend on the Revolution of 1848 in words which we can apply to the pragmatist: " Après avoir beaucoup crié, nous finîmes par en appeler tous les deux à l'avenir, juge éclairé et intègre, mais qui arrive, hélas ! toujours trop tard " (*Souvenirs d'Alexis de Tocqueville*, p. 198 ; quoted by Dicey, *Law and Opinion in England*, p. xxiv).

has been made possible through the previous elaborations of mathematical systems without any obviously direct practical application.[1]   For instance, the first important use for conic sections was found by Kepler after they had been studied for their intrinsic interest for 1,800 years.[2]   He therefore draws two conclusions: (*a*) that the free play of imaginative thought is an ultimate element in the good life (he considers that we have a strong moral intuition of this—witness the almost religious demand for freedom of thought); (*b*) that this will in the long run probably have important consequences in furthering the ends of the Practical Reason, although more valuable results are likely to be arrived at when

---

[1]   A biologist has suggested to me that the reason why Biology at the present day is a backward science relatively to Physics is that its theoretical side is much less developed.   It remains largely a mass of unorganised observations and experiments. Physics, on the other hand, through its closer association with mathematics, can have a highly developed speculative side which gradually finds important applications.   He also suggested that further progress in some problems of Biology was waiting until biologists were ready to speculate with greater boldness about *e.g.* different possible types of living organisms.   (See also J. H. Woodger, *Biological Principles* [London, 1929], pp. 268-272 and *passim*, for a plea for a philosophical criticism of the logical foundations of their own science on the part of biologists, together with a readiness to explore other possibilities in interpretation.)

[2]   *Function of Reason*, p. 59.

the Speculative Reason can work with a certain freedom and detachment than when it is under the stress of practical necessity. As he says in one of his essays on " The Aims of Education," it is less true to say that necessity is the mother of invention than that it is the mother of futile dodges.

These different criteria of the logical scheme taken together assert that it is the aim of the Speculative Reason to arrive at a system of general ideas which will be applicable over the whole of experience. This test is obviously impossible to apply; but the test of any scheme, so far as it goes, is whether it is applicable over certain items of experience, does not clash with other items, and can maintain itself against possible future experience. This seems impossible to satisfy positively, and so it is; nevertheless progress in the history of thought has come from holding it as an operative ideal, regulating the reason, and so preserving " the rational sanity of imaginative thought." Progress in metaphysics can be defined as " an asymptotic approach to a scheme of principles only definable in terms of the ideal which they should satisfy."[1]

The difficulty lies not only in the exact formulation of first principles, insuperably difficult though this may be. The greater difficulty

[1] *Process and Reality*, p. 5 (6).

arises from the fact that the properties of the scheme, as they have been described, are not, as the Greeks and Scholastics may have thought, easy to apply. The field of application must be the whole of experience, and we start from a fragmentary experience as given. That is to say, the method of procedure is not, as might have been expected, deductive. We do not start from certain principles which are clear and distinct, and go on to deduce a system of thought from them, and then see if we can apply it. This may be the method of procedure in mathematics, but it will not do for metaphysics. This has been the mistake philosophy has often made in the past—to assume (as for instance it was assumed in the Cartesian discussions of perception) that experience starts from certain elements which are clear and distinct and easily recognisable. Instead, as Whitehead insists in his discussions of perception, what is prior in consciousness is not prior in time, and very rarely in importance. For experience comes to us, as William James says, as " a big buzzing confusion," and the task of metaphysics is to try and discover whether there are any general characteristics, permanent features, in the welter and confusion.

So Whitehead, though in many respects he is employing the methods of Cartesian rationalism, is very far from being a dogmatist. For dogmatism holds that the basic elements in experience are those which are clear and distinct; whereas he is maintaining that the basic elements are the most elusive. It is a mistake to think that even science starts from a few clear and distinct notions, and proceeds by elaboration of detail. In fact a science can reach a very advanced stage, and the delimitation of its basic notions still be a matter of the utmost difficulty. An obvious example would be the enormous success and mass of manipulative knowledge achieved by modern physics, compared with the widespread indecision and difference of opinion as to its primary notions.

When we apply this principle to metaphysics, it becomes clear that the formulation of a scheme of first principles which will be " the accurate expression of the final generalities " will be " the goal of discussion and not its origin."[1] Metaphysics must not be misled by the example of mathematics. Its primary method is not deduction, but *descriptive generalisation*. By descriptive generalisation is meant arriving at the general ideas which are implicit in our interpretations of experience; making them explicit, and bringing them out into the open, putting them together, and seeing whether they appear consistent and reasonable; in other words, the

---

[1] *Process and Reality*, p. 10 (12).

discovery of the ultimate assumptions implied in all our acting and thinking. If we push this process back as far as it will go, we come finally to certain assumptions for which no further reason outside themselves can be given. If these were really ultimate and necessary, their precise formulation in a scheme in which their mutual implication would be apparent (we here recall the ideal of coherence) would be the goal of our metaphysical enquiry. This is the meaning of the statement at the end of *Process and Reality*, i., § 1, that the " doctrine of necessity in universality means that there is an essence in the universe which forbids relationships beyond itself as a violation of its rationality. Speculative philosophy seeks that essence." This is why, as we are further told,[1] " in all philosophic theory there is an ultimate which is actual in virtue of its accidents." I must leave the fuller discussion of what this means, and a difficulty which will be apparent in the use of the term " accidents " until I come to the notions of " God " and " Creativity." All that is important at present is to notice that we must say that in the end metaphysical speculation will be driven to a first principle, or group of first principles for which no reason beyond themselves can be given, and which will therefore form the " ultimate

[1] *Op. cit.*, p. 9 (10).

irrationality " on which everything also depends.[1]
The reason why all metaphysical systems break
down in the end is that they do not push this
process far enough back; they find their ultimate
irrationality somewhere short of complete generality. (The concept of Substance and Accident
would be an example of this.)

But, at the same time, the fact that all these
systems do look for wider generalities, do try to
push beyond the bounds of merely particular
experience, and attempt some more comprehensive view, means that even if they are never
final, they all tell us something. For the essence
of rationalism is generality, so that whenever we
seek to give a rational explanation, we have said
something about the nature of things, and so have
generalised. We start from a particular, fragmentary experience, and, in seeking to make it,
as we say, significant to ourselves, we commit

---

[1] It might be suggested that this is just a restatement of the
Aristotelian view of knowledge as proceeding from first principles intuitively grasped by νοῦς. But the difference is clear
on reflection ; the first principles grasped by νοῦς are axiomatic,
and certain, and the starting-points for the Discursive Reason
(λόγος). On the view of philosophic method here described,
the principles are not certain nor obvious, and are simply the
furthest we have been able to go in arriving at more general
ideas. So " Metaphysical categories are not dogmatic statements
of the obvious ; they are tentative formulations of the ultimate
generalities " (op. cit., p. 11 [12]).

ourselves to generalising, by using concepts which connect it with other possible experience.[1]

All explanation is therefore, in Bacon's fine phrase, a " looking abroad into universality." Philosophical generalisation simply carries this one stage further.   It starts from some particular field of experience—just what field would not seem to matter; we may say that it can start from anything that is vivid and interesting to us, and which we want to understand more fully; it may be nature, sense-perception, æsthetics, religion, politics, physics, social relationships, history. And when anyone goes deeply enough into any of these, or into any of the many kinds of experience which can become a vital and abiding interest, philosophy is helped forward.   For if there is a sincere and profound desire to understand their significance, it must lead to a perception of these particular experiences, as exemplifying principles which have a wider sweep of application.[2]   The apparent triviality of some of the experiences is not the point; the important thing is to have gone deeply enough into them

[1] The justification of this is another matter, and it must be postponed to Chapter VII.   It turns, clearly enough, on our view of Induction.   All that can be said here is that whatever may be the logical justification of this, the use of present experience to tell us something about experience we have not got is what we are forced to do whenever we generalise.

[2] Cf. *Science and the Modern World*, p. 17.

to see the general principle involved. Examples from the poets of how " to see a world in a grain of sand " are too numerous to quote—we can all recall them for ourselves. Perhaps most famous of them all, we may recall the way in which the Ancient Mariner is brought to see the Love of God and all His creatures from watching the play of water snakes—" happy living things." And there is a whole philosophy of all things in heaven and earth and under the earth drawn out of whaling in Melville's *Moby Dick*.

" What are the Rights of Man and the Liberties of the World but Loose-Fish ? What all men's minds and opinions but Loose-Fish ? What is the principle of religious belief in them but a Loose-Fish ? What to the ostentatious smuggling verbalists are the thoughts of thinkers but Loose-Fish ? What is the great globe itself but a Loose-Fish ? And what are you, reader, but a Loose-Fish and a Fast-Fish too ?"

We must return from this digression to Whitehead's view of philosophic generalisation— but is it a digression after all, when we read that by philosophic generalisation is meant " the utilization of specific notions applying to a re-stricted group of facts, for the divination of the generic notions which apply to all facts "?[1] The attempt at philosophical explanation is, therefore,

[1] *Process and Reality*, p. 6 (8).

"a voyage towards the larger generalities."[1]
These attempts are all illuminating as far as they
go, as they serve to bring into relief some features
in our experience.    They are an advance towards
some sort of synoptic vision, but they break down
when they are applied without qualification
beyond certain limits.    This does not mean that
they are false; they are only unguardedly stated,
and only apply within certain limits; so that they
are not so much disproved as superseded.    It
should therefore be the aim of anyone who tries
to formulate a scheme of ideas to show clearly the
limits within which it is applicable, the point
where it falls short of wider generality, and where
it is in itself inadequate and inconsistent.    It
then becomes more possible for those who come
after to try to correct its deficiencies by a more
comprehensive scheme.    Instead, however, as
Whitehead points out, the natural tendency of a
thinker is to make a scheme appear more adequate
than it is, and perhaps unconsciously hide its
loose ends; so that the weak arguments in his
scheme will not be discovered for several generations.    Moreover, he points out the tendency
of a scheme (such as Aristotle's Logic) which is
too perfect within its limits to stultify thought,
because it comes to be accepted as final.    This
is particularly disastrous when a scheme acquires

[1] *Op. cit.*, p. 12 (14).

orthodoxy, and appeals to any other authority than that of its intrinsic reasonableness. The danger of this, the fact that a philosophical system can appeal to the longing for stability and security, to our natural readiness to treat philosophy as a " Quest for Certainty," and so even as a way of escape from the storms and stress of the contemporary world, makes many feel that Whitehead is gravely mistaken in holding that the systematic method is the right one in metaphysics.[1] But must the dangers of the method mean that it is necessarily wrong ? *Corruptio optimi pessima.* The danger lies in treating as static and final what is only the temporary and tentative result reached at any time by the Speculative Reason in its never-ending adventure towards the discovery of more adequate general ideas. And Whitehead maintains again and again that the evidence of the history of thought goes to show that " the secret of progress is the speculative interest in abstract schemes of morphology "; that " the development of abstract theory precedes the understanding of fact."[2] For better or worse, above all through the embodiment of their ideas in institutions, systems of thought have played an incalculable part in the

[1] This objection, I would suggest, is based generally on psychological grounds rather than on the philosophical grounds examined in the next chapter.

[2] See especially *Function of Reason*, pp. 58-59.

growth of civilization.   Nor can it fairly be said
that Whitehead fails to see their dangers, as well
as their value.

" A system of dogmas may be the ark within
which the Church floats safely down the flood-
tide of history.   But the Church will perish
unless it opens its windows and lets out the dove
to search for an olive branch.   Sometimes even
it will do well to disembark on Mount Ararat
and build a new altar to the divine Spirit, an altar
neither in Mount Gerizim nor yet at Jerusalem."[1]

" There is a greatness in the lives of those who
build up religious systems, a greatness in action,
in idea and in self-subordination, embodied in instance after instance through centuries of growth.
There is a greatness in the rebels who destroy
such systems: they are the Titans who storm
heaven, armed with passionate sincerity."[2]

And the final answer to those who maintain
that because it is clearly not the business of every
student of philosophy to have a complete system
of ideas (the necessary comprehensive knowledge,
and the capacity for sustained and constructive
thought will be a very rare thing), the time has
gone when any philosopher should try, is given
in the third of the statements quoted at the
beginning of this chapter.   " All constructive

[1] *Religion in the Making* (Cambridge, 1926), pp. 145-146.
[2] *Process and Reality*, p. 478 (513).

thought . . . is dominated by some such scheme, unacknowledged, but no less influential in guiding the imagination. The importance of philosophy lies in its sustained effort to make such schemes explicit, and thereby capable of criticism and improvement."

If, therefore, those who formulate systems of ideas can show clearly the limits within which they are applicable and the point at which they break down, they can all be of value in elucidating something. For "a new idea introduces a new alternative; and we are not less indebted to a thinker when we adopt the alternative which he discarded. Philosophy never reverts to its old position after the shock of a great philosopher."[1] We may recall the words about Bentham in J. S. Mill's *Essay on Coleridge*:[2] "A true thinker can only be justly estimated when his thoughts have worked their way into minds formed in a different school: have been wrought and moulded into consistency with all other true and relevant thoughts; when the noisy conflict of half-truths, angrily denying one another, has subsided and ideas which seemed mutually incompatible have been found only to require mutual limitations."

But all systems tend to claim a wider application than that to which they are entitled. Within certain abstract limits, systems like scientific

---

[1] *Op. cit.*, p. 14 (16).
[2] *Dissertations and Discussions*, vol. i.

mechanism or the materialist conception of history are not false (and indeed they bear abundant witness at any rate to the fighting power of abstract general ideas) ; but they are often unguardedly stated as if they were the whole truth. This suggests the Idealist theory of error, as expounded, for instance, in Professor Joachim's book *The Nature of Truth*. Error is there the claim of an abstract, partial truth to be wholly true. I am not convinced that this is the whole story about error in judgments (in fact I find myself in complete agreement with the greater part of Russell's criticism of it in his *Philosophical Essays*); but it very fairly expresses this view of the truth and falsity of philosophical systems.

People seem to have a deep-rooted love of generalising their ideas; perhaps from the right perception that what is true for one should be true for all. But the result is that those who live within a certain system of ideas are apt to be unable to look beyond it, and so we find an over-emphasis and parochialism in the specialised departments of thought, for instance in science, economics or theology. There is a tendency in specialised thought to over-emphasise the importance of its particular general ideas, and to assume that they ought to be of universal application.[1]

[1] The tragedy this can mean when those ideas are clearly no longer adequate and have lost their appeal to intrinsic reason-

This is because conscious thought is essentially selective; it picks out certain features in the totality of experience and raises them into relief. So in every department of thought there is an element of subjective over-emphasis. It is the business of philosophy to correct this subjectivity; to restore " the balance of importance disclosed in the rational vision."[1] This is what Whitehead calls the morality of rationality. " Morality of outlook is inseparably conjoined with generality of outlook. The antithesis between the general good and the individual interest can be abolished only when the individual is such that its interest is the general good, thus exemplifying the loss of the minor intensities in order to find them again with finer composition in a wider sweep of interest."[2] We have here a connection between the nature of rationality and what we shall see is one of the basic conceptions of the Philosophy of Organism. Nor is the idea a new one; indeed it is probably as old as philosophy. And it finds another setting in Kant's discovery of the mutual implication of the notions of rationality, morality, universality and freedom.

But the problem of metaphysics lies precisely in the fact that it is trying to discover general

---

ableness, and so bolster themselves up with some kind of authority, is described in Edmund Gosse's *Father and Son*.

[1] *Process and Reality*, p. 20 (23).                    [2] *Ibid.*

principles which are universally applicable; and, as Whitehead says in ch. i., § 2., there is nothing so difficult as to see what is always there.   This is because we notice and perceive things by the method of difference—"the object observed is important when present and sometimes is absent." But the metaphysical first principles can never fail of exemplification, and so we cannot notice them by their absence.[1]   In other words, they

---

[1] *Cf.* Aristotle, *Met.*, A (992$^b$24).   πῶς δ'ἄν τις καὶ μάθοι τὰ τῶν πάντων στοιχεῖα ;   We cannot know the universal elements in all things, because we have no means of defining them, or premises from which to start.   Aristotle is attacking Plato's dialectic, as a science which will deduce the concrete nature of reality from certain principles common to all reality.

See Mr. Ross's note, in his commentary on the *Metaphysics* (Oxford, 1924), vol. i., p. 210.   The distinction drawn is between dialectic, as a science which will deduce the concrete nature of reality from the first principles of all things, and metaphysics as the study of the general nature of anything which is said to "be."   The concrete nature of reality can only be got at by reflection on the principles peculiar to its various departments, and on particular perceptions.

F. R. Tennant, *Philosophical Theology* (Cambridge, 1930), vol. ii., p. 155, calls attention to the way in which while "the potential Aristotle saw that philosophy involves tentative procedure from the confusedly but better and earlier known to the more adequately but later known, from common sense and special sciences to 'first philosophy,'" the actual Aristotle (and, we may add, still more his followers) forsook this method for unproved speculation, and hence lost centuries of what might have been constructive philosophy.

are so obvious that we fail to see them. This means they are not to be found by direct observation. They are not essentially unknowable: they may be arrived at by a flash of imaginative insight; but it is doubtful whether in fact we can get beyond " an asymptotic approach to a scheme of principles, only definable in terms of the ideal which they should satisfy."[1]

But when we have arrived by imagination, reflection and criticism at some notion of what these general principles may be, then we must bring them out into the open, try and see whether they form a coherent scheme, and then go back and see whether this scheme helps to elucidate our experience. Whitehead calls this scheme "categorical." He puts out his own categorical scheme in *Process and Reality*, chapter ii.; and the rest of the book is concerned with its elucidation and application. He is obviously not proceeding deductively; that is, he did not first formulate the scheme, and then see what followed from it, but only came to formulate the scheme as the result of

[1] How this might be conceived is suggested by A. E. Taylor, in *The Faith of a Moralist* (London, 1930), ii., pp. 409-412. It is a " rationalisation " which can never finally be completed. but which interprets reality by a theory in principle like the valuation of a surd, *e.g.*, $\sqrt{2}$. This is ἄλογον, but yet we can find an unending series of fractions such that the product of any term by itself is more nearly equal to 2 than that of any of its precursors by itself.

the reflections contained in the rest of his work. But he here puts out the scheme at the beginning, and the reader is faced with the difficulty that while the ideas contained in it are practically unintelligible apart from the rest of the book, at the same time the book is unintelligible apart from the scheme. The only way, therefore, is to take the book and scheme together; and after several readings hope that they will throw light on each other. I will not say that this is a very satisfactory way of writing a philosophy book; and it will perhaps not commend itself to very many. But it has one great advantage, in that the writer has put out his cards on the table at the outset, and has given a definite statement of his categorical notions to which we can refer. It is no doubt a method which comes naturally to a mathematician. He is putting forward his postulates without any apology or explanation, and is looking to the rest of the book to justify and elucidate them. The test therefore will be whether the rest of the work, especially where it seems to be valuable and illuminating, can be shown to be in any direct relation to the principles set out in the scheme; and whether these principles do really become clear and find their application as the book goes on.

*Note on Whitehead's Terminology.*—A further difficulty in understanding the categorical scheme, or indeed any of Whitehead's work, lies in his use of words. We noted a short way back, in connection with the requirements of a philosophical scheme, that clarity of propositional content is to be sought through formulating a language which will avoid the ambiguities of ordinary language. Whitehead extends this principle to claim that the modern philosopher has the right to coin new words when he wishes to express a new idea, since he holds that many of the old philosophical terms are now misleading in their associations. Moreover, the vagueness and unanalysed associations of ordinary language are obviously something of real value in literature and poetry, but misleading in philosophy. It may well be that in contrast with the way in which a literary language reproduces the living, concrete flow of experience, we may feel a certain barbarity about the abstractions of the philosopher. For " Who can find a language for this difference, for this elusiveness ? Or if words are found for the outer form, they are the terms of a new science; a speech which has never fought under a master of writing, never learned the ways of an old society. . . . Who can read Whitehead's *Science and the Modern World* without thinking of those armies of men with eastern helmets and new shaped swords who came through the Caucasian passes with Jenghis Khan ? These

4

invaders are here now to settle as well as to over-throw."[1]   Yet Whitehead claims that, in the interests of clarity of propositional content, he must have considerable freedom in making new words to express new shades of meaning without ambiguity, even at the cost of initial obscurity. We may recall the remark of Berkeley's Philonous, which he sets at the beginning of *The Principles of Natural Knowledge*.[2]   " I am not for imposing any sense on your words: you are at liberty to explain them as you please.   Only I beseech you, make me understand something by them."

But the result is a certain added difficulty in understanding him at first, or indeed second reading, since he is apt to have an almost entirely new vocabulary of technical words in each book, and to plunge us into it with very little in the way of definition or explanation.   Hence the meaning of a good many of his terms—not so much of his new technical words, but the precise meaning he is giving to old words, such as " God," " Feeling," " Reason "—can only be made clear by an understanding of the thought of the whole book; while the thought can only be understood by means of the terms.   The only way, therefore, is to notice continually the exact words he is using (perhaps to make one's own glossary of

[1] E. L. Woodward, *The Twelve-Winded Sky*, p. 4.
[2] Cambridge, 1919.

them) and then, after several readings, the meaning of the thought and of the terms may gradually become clear in the light of each other. Very often the meaning he is giving to a word can be found from its exact etymological sense; and it is some of these terms which I feel are among his happiest, and which are likely to be a real gain to our philosophical vocabulary. Examples are: (*a*) Concrescence, from *concrescere*, meaning the process of many diversities growing together into a new unity, which at the culmination of the process is a fully-developed thing, and so concrete (*concretum*). (*b*) Prehension, as a general word for the grasping, or taking hold of one thing by another, and so connoting an active coming together, which the word " relation," with its suggestions of a static morphology, fails to express; while " apprehension " suggests consciousness. (*c*) Ingression, for the entry of a form into the constitution of an actuality, so that it becomes an " ingredient " in it. (*d*) Decision, in its root sense of a " cutting off," applied to an actuality as the definite realising of one, and exclusion of other possible alternatives. These terms will all need further elucidation as the notions they express come up for discussion; and other terms of a similar description will be noticed.

# CHAPTER III

## SOME CHALLENGES TO "THE SENTIMENT OF RATIONALITY"

Philosophy,
shuttling out in the unknown like a hungry spider,
blindly spinneth her geometric webs, testing
and systematizing even her own disorders.
*The Testament of Beauty.*

Prospero's island—the integration into the everlastingly valid frame of things of unaccommodated waifs from alien shores—is the compendium and symbol of a process of immense significance.—J. L. Lowes : *The Road to Xanadu.*

THE mention of Kant towards the end of the last chapter must have suggested a doubt which may long before have entered the reader's mind. What of all this talk about the Speculative Reason; this assertion that there is still a place for pure metaphysics, with its ideal of a rational scheme ? Has Whitehead fairly faced the problem set by the Critical Philosophy, the question as to whether the necessary logical laws of our reason are also the laws of things; the whole problem in fact of the relation of thought to reality which was set so forcibly by Kant, and afterwards by Bradley ? Shall we not be forced to agree with a review of *Process and Reality* by John Dewey, and "close the book with the feeling that somehow the seventeenth century has got the better of the twentieth"?

The first answer is that there is a sense in which Whitehead would acknowledge this himself, since he explicitly says that, in the main, "the philosophy of organism is a recurrence to pre-Kantian modes of thought."[1] In saying this, he is protesting against what he says has been the effect of the Critical Philosophy in driving a wedge between science and the speculative reason. The post-Kantian Idealist tradition, by emphasising the distinction between the abstract universal of science and the search for the concrete universal in philosophy and history, has turned philosophy into a critical reflection on subjective experience. Giving up, as the result of Kant's attacks, the attempt to find an order in *things*, the mind has turned in on itself, and sought an order in its own experiences as thinking and willing.[2] Kant showed, probably once for all, that in natural knowledge we can never get away from sense-perception. But his successors in the Idealist school were too far removed from the scientific outlook for their theories to have much bearing on the specula-

---

[1] *Process and Reality*, p. vi.

[2] And some would say that it is being driven from even this last stronghold by psychology.

tive side of science. In *Science and the Modern World*[1] Whitehead traced this divergence of the Idealist tradition from science, and the consequent contentment of scientists with a materialist cosmology, from the Cartesian view of two kinds of Substance—cogitating mind and extended matter. Philosophic Idealism then took charge of cogitating mind, and science of extended matter. The effort to combine these two makes science the mere study of phenomena in a phenomenal world, of which all we can say in the end is that its truths are not very true, and that they throw no light upon metaphysics. But the result of this is either to leave us with an Unknowable Reality (and an incidental difficulty here is that philosophers cannot leave it simply unknown, but then seem to find themselves called upon to make all sorts of statements about it); or there is recourse to some view of another way of knowing, since science tells us nothing whatever about the nature of things. So Kant found an escape from mere phenomenalism in the requirements of the Practical Reason; Eddington finds one in " mysticism."

The dilemma in which this leaves us has, like so many of these things, been put inimitably in *The Testament of Beauty*:[2]

[1] Pp. 193-194, 202.
[2] I., ll. 350 *sq.*

As a man thru' a window into a darken'd house
peering vainly wil see, always and easily,
the glass surface and his own face mirror'd thereon. . . .
See how they hav made o' the window an impermeable wall
partitioning man off from the rest of nature
with stronger impertinence than Science can allow.[1]
Man's mind, Nature's entrusted gem, her own mirror
cannot bë isolated from her other works
by self-abstraction of its unique fecundity
in the new realm of his transcendent life.

If science is an intellectual interest of merely
subjective importance, or if its symbolism bears
no relation whatever to the structure of that
which it symbolises, how can it even be " practical " or convenient ? Whitehead continually
insists that we must be on our guard against any
view which reduces science to a mere subjective
day-dream with a taste of the day-dream for
publication. For scientific explanation is always
a generalisation, and he holds that whenever
we generalise, whether our propositions be true
or false, we are asserting something about the
nature of things. If this is so, science, as even
Wordsworth saw, can become more than a tool
of the dissecting intellect, for

taught with patient interest to watch
The processes of things, and serve the cause

[1] For, as Whitehead says in *The Concept of Nature* (Cambridge, 1926), p. 27, this in the end " has transformed the grand question of the relations between nature and mind into the petty form of the interaction between the human body and mind."

Of order and distinctness, not for this
Shall it forget that its most noble use,
Its most illustrious province, must be found
In furnishing clear guidance, a support
Not treacherous, to the mind's *excursive* power.

Whitehead therefore protests against any view which rigidly divides categorical knowledge, which tells us something of reality, from science, which consists in pseudo-concepts, or purely practical and manipulative knowledge. He is maintaining the old Cartesian point of view, that all " clear and distinct " thought tells us *something*, though *what* may be vastly more difficult to determine than Descartes ever dreamt. That is to say, he is claiming to follow the Platonic intellectualist tradition, that there is a real affinity between the Reason in us, and the structure, which is an objective λόγος, in the nature of things. He is holding that the true Apostolic succession in metaphysics has been from Plato and Aristotle, through a certain part of Christian Theology, in so far as it has been a development from Greek Philosophy, and through the philosophers from Descartes to Hume; that Kantian and Hegelian Idealism has been a digression, albeit an extremely valuable critical digression, but that the time has now come when we should return to the main stream. The main characteristics of this stream I will suggest to be the following:

(*a*) An interest in speculative metaphysics, and a belief in its possibility and necessity as an imaginative enquiry into the ultimate questions concerning Being and Nature. (In this it will be concerned with the questions which arise from an attempt to understand the order of the world, and the mystery of what Whitehead calls " the ideal opposites, Permanence and Flux, the One and the Many.")

(*b*) Its close association with scientific thought, resulting from the belief that, on the one hand, the advance of scientific knowledge may throw light on philosophical problems; and on the other hand, that the construction of a cosmology, a *de rerum natura*, elucidating the general ideas underlying the sciences, is part of the essential work of philosophy.

(*c*) An interest in mathematics, and in problems of order and structure. Allied with this, there is a tendency to look for a connection between this kind of reasoning, and ethics and æsthetics; to find a relation between the appreciation of the beauty of the exactness of things, and a moral intuition of rightness, rather than to consider these branches of experience as *sui generis*.

It may be that, in returning to this type of thought, Whitehead has insufficiently allowed for the difficulties which were put by the Critical Philosophy; the question as to what evidence

4 *

we have that things must conform to the ways in which we seek to make them intelligible to ourselves.   We must now briefly consider what may be said in his defence.

The abiding value of the Kantian philosophy lies in the discovery that an act of experience is a process of construction.[1]   But according to Kant, the objective world is constructed by the subject experiencing; while in Whitehead's Philosophy of Organism the experiencing subject arises out of the world which it feels, and constructs its own nature from the way in which it feels it. Which way round is most likely to be right ?

Perhaps the major problem in the Kantian view may be put by asking from whence does the knowing subject get the categories ?   If they anticipate all experience, the only possible answer is that it is eternally endowed with them.   But this commits us to a view of the mind as an Athene springing ready armed from the head of Zeus; and since the *a priori* is before all experience, we cannot even say that it would be the logical structure of any developed mind.   The fact of course is that the notion of a mind as growing and constructing itself is foreign to Kant's view of noumenal reality.   If however we are to take seriously the side of his philosophy where he describes the mind as a synthesising activity,

[1] *Process and Reality*, p. 217 (236).

we may say that the *a priori* is the formal scheme which it uses to delimit reality, or, in other words, to make its experience intelligible. The categories are then criteria of interpretation for *veridical* experience—not the formal element in all possible experience, since dreams and illusions and unconscious feelings, which do not always come to us in terms of the categories, are none the less experience. Moreover we might argue that the categories are only criteria of veridical experience so long as they prove themselves adequate to be such, and so long as we are prepared to maintain them. They are a net in which we try the experiment of catching the real; and when the real eludes us, we gradually come to amend our categories. It is doubtful whether all of Kant's categories, for instance that of Substance, could any longer be accepted as concepts necessary for the possibility of experience.

The point is that the logical priority of the categories, as formal criteria, is entirely compatible with a shift in our notion of them from a widening of our knowledge. The categories might therefore be said to be used by the mind as the most adequate criteria of veridical experience it has as yet formed.[1]

[1] I have drawn the greater part of this view of the *a priori* from C. I. Lewis's *Mind and the World Order* (New York, 1929), from which the following quotation is also taken. I am greatly indebted to this book. It should perhaps be pointed out that

This would depend upon the way in which the " given " manifold of experience most readily permits itself to be ordered by these conceptual schemes; and therefore we might say that as the schemes show themselves more adequate for interpreting experience, they are following more closely the connections, or "laws " in the structure of what is given.   So " the determination of reality, the classification of phenomena, and the discovery of law, all grow up together."   This sounds like asking Kant to give up his Copernican hypothesis; but this would only follow in so far as, as James Ward said, " In claiming that reason (*sic*) must be *aut Cæsar aut nullus* he spoiled a good case for a constitutional monarchy."[1]   The Copernican hypothesis would still stand as the insistence which Kant made so forcibly, and probably once for all, on there being a subjective as well as an objective element in all knowing.   For " Beyond such

---

by " veridical " is here meant " non-illusory," in the sense of " controlled by the real."   Kant indeed says at the beginning of the Transcendental Deduction (see *Analytic of Concepts*, ch. ii., §i., p. 124 in Professor Kemp Smith's translation, London, 1929) that the categories are necessary to show " how subjective conditions of thought can have objective validity."   " For appearances can certainly be given in intuition independent of functions of the understanding."   But by " objectively valid '' Kant means falling within the unity of apperception (cf. *ibid.*, pp. 144 *sq.*).   This is not synonymous with " veridical " as here understood in Lewis's realistic sense.

[1] J. Ward, *A Study in Kant* (Cambridge, 1922), p. 60.

principles as those of logic and pure mathematics whose permanent stability seems attested, there must be further and more particular criteria of the real prior to any investigation of nature. Such definitions, fundamental principles and criteria the mind itself must supply before experience can even begin to be intelligible. These represent more or less deep-lying attitudes which the human mind has taken in the light of its total experience up to date. But a newer and wider experience may bring about some alteration of these attitudes even though by themselves they dictate nothing as to the content of experience, and no experience can conceivably prove them invalid."[1] Not invalid, perhaps, but certainly inadequate, and so they will gradually be superseded and abandoned. And the test of adequacy, except in the rare instance of an intuitive judgment of the exact fit of a concept with " given " experience, must, it seems, be pragmatic (using the term simply to denote a method of testing, and realising that even as a test it is tentative and never final).

If, therefore, we revert to the question as to which way round we are to take the Kantian view that an act of experience is a construction, it looks as though this view of the categories favoured the construction as being that of the subject from the way in which it tries to feel and know its

[1] C. I. Lewis, *op. cit.*, pp. 265-266.

given world, rather than as that of the objective world according to laws prescribed by the subject. The subject's conceptual scheme is not a condition of the possibility of experience, but the means by which it seeks to delimit and interpret its veridical experience. It arrives at this scheme by forming the most adequate general ideas it can of the kind of connections which may exist in the nature of the " given," and so the way in which it may be most amenable to interpretation. Thus we come round to Whitehead's view of the nature of a metaphysical scheme, as the elucidation of the general ideas necessary for classifying and determining what is real.

This means that, instead of the view of consciousness as prior, and as legislating the principles of possible experience, we have to look on a mind as arising out of the background of its given world, and progressively constructing its own concepts according to the kind of connection which it finds, or expects to find, in its world, which connections it tries to express in symbolic form. A view of the property of a symbol if it is to bear a relation to the symbolised has been stated by Wittgenstein. It seems to fit those symbols Peirce called " eikons," but not those that, for example, name something. The proposition is called " ein Masstab an die Wirklichkeit angelegt " —a scale applied to reality—and its logical form

must exhibit a logical articulation in the thing symbolised.[1] "At first glance the proposition, say
as it stands printed on paper does not seem to be
a picture of the reality of which it treats. But nor
does the musical score appear at first sight to be a
picture of a musical piece; nor does our phonetic
spelling seem to be a picture of our spoken
language. And yet these symbolisms prove to
be pictures. . . . The gramophone record, the
musical thought, the score, the waves of sound,
all stand to one another in that pictorial internal
relation which holds between language and the
world. To all of them the logical structure is
common." (*Cf.* 4.023: "The proposition constructs a world with the help of a logical scaffold-
ing, and therefore one can actually see in the
proposition all the logical features possessed by
reality if it is true.")

We come back, therefore, to the Platonic principle that if any rational understanding is to be
possible, the λόγος in us must be akin to a λόγος
in things.[2] And here it looks as though we must

[1] *Tractatus,* 4.01-4.06.

[2] I would like to suggest that one of the ways in which
Descartes returned to the Platonic tradition from the Aristotel-
ianism of the Middle Ages, was in invoking this principle, though
in a more misleading form. The appeal to God's not being
a cheat and deceiver, in order to establish the validity of his
reason, is only not a circular argument if we look on it as the
assertion that the validity of our reason in telling us anything

take our choice.   We must either say that *no* intellectual understanding of the world is possible, that reason can tell us nothing whatever about the nature of things, and so be frank anti-intellectualists; or we can make the postulate that there is a logical structure in reality, and that rationalism is a never-ending adventure in trying to approximate more nearly to an adequate symbolic formulation of it.   This may simply (to quote once more from the passage in *Science and the Modern World*)[1] be " faith in reason " as " the trust that the ultimate natures of things lie together in a harmony which excludes mere arbitrariness," " the faith that at the base of things we shall not find mere arbitrary mystery."   Yet if this is an ungrounded faith, a mere clinging to the comfortable security afforded by the Sentiment of Rationality, it is hard to see why, as is undoubtedly the case, the great creative achievements of civilization, science (even in the sense simply of manipulative knowledge), perhaps we may say, of all that makes man most characteristically human, have been built upon it.

Yet for this intellectual laughter—deem it not
true Wisdom's panoply.  The wise wil live by Faith,
faith in the order of Nature and that her order is good.[2]

---

about the nature of things, and the existence of an objective Reason in things themselves, stand and fall together.

[1] P. 26.          [2] *Testament of Beauty*, I., ll. 561-563.

But there is a further difficulty in holding that there can be any valid correspondence between the schematisms of thought and the reality they try to symbolise, which, like Kant's difficulties, goes deeper than the objections of any lightly held anti-intellectualism or romanticism. It is the difficulty which was seen and expressed in different ways by Bradley, Bergson and Croce. Thought is necessarily relational, and it must analyse its object in a static morphology of terms and relations; whereas reality itself is to be looked upon as what Professor J. A. Smith describes as a "seamless whole," a living and concrete experience. So there will necessarily always be a misfit between the abstract spatialising intellect and the reality it tries to understand. This indeed is a challenge to the whole Platonic view of a valid relation between thought and reality.

Bradley's view is based on the argument that thought is relational, and what is relational is self-contradictory and therefore not true.[1] Thought he sees must be relational; it cannot grasp the concrete unity of anything, or it would include feeling and cease to be mere thinking. So "the relational form is a compromise on which thought stands and which it develops. It is an attempt to unite differences which have broken

[1] *Appearance and Reality* (2nd edition, London, 1897), ch. xv., pp. 171-180; and also ch. iii.

out of the felt totality." But if the differences are united as they are in the seamless whole of reality, "they would perish and their relation would perish with them." They would be absorbed in a fuller experience which would be, not thought, but feeling. The Real is that which is whole, and not in relation; while thought puts asunder what reality has joined. To know the Absolute, it would be necessary fully to feel the Absolute, and then thought, and even knowledge, as it involves an otherness of knower and known, would be superseded.

But the insuperable objection to this view is that thought, however relational and abstract, does tell us *something*. Or how is it that when we are dissatisfied with our perception of the real by immediate feeling, we turn away to abstract analytical thought, and then come back again to a richer and fuller feeling? An example would be the way in which when we hear a piece of music after studying the score we really do, as we say, hear more and hear it better than before. Neither Bradley's view of degrees of truth and reality in " mere appearance " (so long at any rate as he still takes seriously the adjective " mere," and holds to the self-contradictoriness of relational thought), nor Bergson's view of the spatialising intellect as developing in response to practical needs, seems adequately to account for this.[1] Relational thought could tell us nothing, nor even be of practical value, unless its symbolism had some kind of relevant reference to distinctions in the real. If we maintain that it has some such relevance, then we shall say that the reason why thought does make our concrete experience richer and fuller can only be because the abstractions of thought symbolise articulations in the real. The problem then becomes the Platonic one; namely, how it is that concrete fact can exhibit characters which can be described in terms of universals. Concrete fact is not made up simply of universals; this may be allowed, and also the corollary that its total nature could be

---

[1] A. E. Taylor (*Faith of a Moralist*, ii., p. 343) puts well the dilemma with which Bergson's view of knowledge leaves us : " So long as you think, as Bergson does, on the one hand of an actual experience which is sheer qualitative flux and variety, and on the other, of a geometrical ready-made framework of sheer non-qualitative abidingness, there seems no possible answer to the question how *such* a ' matter ' comes to be forced into the strait waistcoat of so inappropriate a ' form,' except to lay the blame on some wilful *culpa originalis* of the intellect." He suggests that Bergson's problem is answered by the theory of relativity, showing that it is impossible to locate an experience in time without reference to space. So the " geometrising " of the intellect consists in the cutting loose of location in time and space from each other, when in actual fact they are given together ; though such separation in thought is necessary for communication. I do not feel certain that Bergson would accept this solution, or whether he would not say that the time which is wedded to space is simply mathematical, " spatialised time."

grasped only in feeling, or in Bergsonian intuition. But thought is an analysis of the formal structure which concrete fact exhibits — in other words "the search for the forms in the facts."

The further implications of what this statement means in Whitehead's philosophy must be left until we come to consider his claim to be called a Platonist. Broadly speaking, it means that he holds that certain elements in the structure of concrete fact can be formally distinguished. (This notion also must await further elucidation in Chapter V.)   In thinking we analyse the ways in which these are related.   Science is therefore called the analysis of the "factors in fact."   The clearest statement of this is found in the chapter on " The Relatedness of Nature " in *The Principle of Relativity*.[1]   A fact is there described as a relationship of factors; and awareness as the consciousness of fact as involving factors, which factors may be prescinded from their background of fact, and considered individually as " entities." " Entities " in this sense are described here, and in *The Concept of Nature*,[2] as factors considered as termini or objectives of thought.   " Red," " round," " three feet square " would be examples. "Thought places before itself bare objectives, entities as we call them, which the thinking clothes by expressing their mutual relations.

[1] Cambridge, 1922.          [2] Pp. 12 *sq.*

Sense-awareness discloses fact with factors which are the entities for thought. The separate distinction of an entity in thought is not a meta-physical assertion, but a method of procedure necessary for the finite expression of individual propositions. Apart from entities there could be no finite truths: they are the means by which the infinitude of irrelevance is kept out of thought."[1]

That is to say, the analysis of a fact in this way is never complete; the totality of factors in fact is inexhaustible. But by distinguishing certain factors, and considering them as entities, *i.e.* as objectives for thought, we can make in-dividual true and false propositions about them; and the possibility of finite truth and falsity in these propositions is secured by our *meaning* in discriminating only these factors, and disregarding the infinity of others as irrelevant to our purpose. Intellectual understanding is the analysis of formal elements in this sense in concrete matters of fact. Whitehead calls this kind of analysis " Co-ordinate Division."[2]

Two further observations may be made with regard to the alleged self-contradictoriness of relational thought. In the first place, Bradley insists that since thought is ideal, it is distinct from its object. The object is therefore an Other which must necessarily fall outside the all-em-

---

[1] *Concept of Nature*, p. 12.  [2] Cf. *infra*, p. 98.

bracing Whole which thought seeks to compass; and we have here a contradiction. But this is only a difficulty so long as we think that the goal of truth is to become an all-inclusive individual, which is the same as reality. If, instead, we accept the situation that thought, as thought, must necessarily be other than its object, we shall see that the question is really one of the nature of symbolism. We then have to ask what should be the properties of anything in order for it to be used as a symbol of something else ?[1]

Secondly there is the suspicion that both Bradley, and Kant before him, have been too ready to ascribe the contradictions they see in pure thought to the nature of thought itself rather than to the inadequacy of our concepts, and particularly of our mathematical concepts. For example, the antinomies formerly found in the notion of the Infinite have now been resolved by more adequate mathematical definitions. Moreover, if we accept the view, which the *Principia Mathematica* set out to prove, that pure mathematics is a part of logic, we can no longer be bound by Kant's view of it as synthetic *a priori* knowledge. Kant held that mathematics involved an intuition of Space and Time as the pure forms of experience. Then alleged contradictions in the notions of Space and Time led

[1] Cf. *supra*, p. 52.

to further antinomies. But the modern logical view claims to deduce the underlying notions of mathematics from the primitive propositions of formal logic. Russell now[1] is prepared to say that the whole of pure mathematics is analytic (*i.e.* derived from logic alone), and so tautological, in the sense in which Wittgenstein defines this word. That is to say, it shows how different sets of symbols are different ways of saying the same thing, or how one set says part of what the other set says. So even if we could be certain that the notions of physical Space and Time involve contradictions, this would be quite irrelevant to the question of whether the pure reason must run into antinomies. The two questions are only connected so long as it is held that mathematics depends upon a pure intuition of Space and Time.[2]

[1] *Analysis of Matter* (London, 1927), pp. 170-171. Russell has apparently changed his view on this point. Cf. *Principles of Mathematics* (Cambridge, 1903), p. 457, and *The Philosophy of Leibniz* (Cambridge, 1900), pp. 16 *sq.* But in these latter passages " analytic " was used to denote propositions in which the predicate is contained in the subject, presupposing the subject-predicate form of statement. It was in this sense that Kant denied $7 + 5 = 12$ to be analytic. Russell now defines analytic propositions as those which can be deduced from logic alone, and therefore as including all propositions of pure mathematics.

[2] See Russell, *The Principles of Mathematics*, ch. lii., and *cf.* F. P. Ramsey, *Foundations of Mathematics* (London, 1931), p. 3. " The theories of the intuitionists admittedly involve

We may now briefly sum up the argument of this chapter as follows:

(*a*) The problem of the relation of thought and reality is seen to centre in the problem of symbolism. Thought must be a symbolic representation of logical forms which correspond to articulations of the real.

(*b*) Our various *a priori* schematisms are progressive attempts to catch the real in some kind of conceptual net.

(*c*) The fact that the real allows itself to be thought about at all, or become in any degree intelligible, suggests that though any particular logical scheme we may formulate is probably very far from being even an approximate representation of its actual structure, yet there must be some points of resemblance. Otherwise it is hard to see how even manipulative knowledge is possible.

(*d*) Therefore important reservations must be made in the view that natural science is purely manipulative knowledge, and tells us nothing whatever of the actual structure of things.

(*e*) The primary link between natural science and philosophy is to be found in mathematics.

---

giving up many of the most fruitful methods of modern analysis, for no reason, as it seems to me, except that the methods fail to conform to their private prejudices. They do not therefore profess to give any foundation for mathematics as we know it, but only for a narrower body of truth which has not yet been clearly defined."

Pure mathematics is a branch of logic, which seeks to formulate a symbolism in which the logical forms of propositions and their implications can be expressed unambiguously. In applied mathematics, some of these forms are seen to be exemplified in the physical field. Moreover, if we can see that one such formal concept is exemplified in an actual occasion, we can know an indefinite number of other formal concepts are implied in it.[1]

(*f*) The category of RELATION becomes of fundamental importance. Science analyses various correlations between certain factors abstracted from concrete fact which may be described as the formal elements in fact. Metaphysics tries to formulate more precisely the essential factors in anything which can be said to be, and to exhibit their relation to one another. Whitehead's Philosophy of Organism is intended to make a contribution towards this.[2]

We may conclude therefore that in claiming the right to go behind Kant, and attack once more the problem of speculative metaphysics, there is enough that can be said in Whitehead's

[1] See *Science and the Modern World*, p. 38. "The key to the patterns means this fact :—that from a select set of those general conditions, exemplified in any one and the same occasion, a pattern involving an infinite variety of other such conditions, also exemplified in the same occasion, can be developed by the pure exercise of abstract logic."

[2] See *Process and Reality*, p. viii (ix).

defence at any rate to make his attempt a legitimate one. And if we can agree broadly with his defence of rationalism, and claim that there is a real relation between the general ideas of his system and some of the flashes of insight which everyone would agree are contained in some of the propositions which follow from it, we shall conclude that a system such as his can have more than simply a psychological or æsthetic value.

We may also reflect that there was no time when this kind of disciplined and sustained constructive thought was more needed. The *Zeitgeist* of much of modern thought might be described as a distrust of general ideas, and a rather pathetic hankering after them; a feeling that the general ideas which have built up our philosophies, our science, our social and religious institutions are no longer applicable; and yet that the world is too complicated for us to be able to find new and more adequate general ideas by which we can live. So we turn to "experimentalism"; or to a philosophy of sensitivity to immediate feeling, which is, after all, simply a new Epicureanism; or to a Stoic disinterestedness, or rather apathy, such as Walter Lippmann describes in his *Preface to Morals*, and which is still more negative.

Of the first, it may be said that there is a true and false experimentalism. There is the true

experimentalism, which refuses to allow us to
let our abstract ideas become inert, by showing
how they can be tested and recast, and bear fruit
in action through the development of creative
intelligence;[1] and there is the false experimentalism of the person who simply talks about the
abstract idea of being experimental, and objects
to other people spending time and interest on
other abstract ideas.

Of the new Epicureanism, it can only be said
that it is no new idea; and that it fails to face the
problem of the right relation of feeling and
reason, freedom and discipline, spontaneity and
self-control, which has been seen by philosophers
and moral and religious teachers all through the
ages. It is brilliantly epitomised in Pater's *Marius
the Epicurean*, in words which are as applicable
today as to the time of which he writes.

" In that age of Marcus Aurelius, so completely
disabused of the metaphysical ambition to pass
beyond ' the flaming ramparts of the world,' but,
on the other hand, possessed of so vast an ac-
cumulation of intellectual treasure, with so wide
a view before it over all varieties of what is power-
ful or attractive in man and his works, the thoughts

---

[1] The fact that John Dewey genuinely lives in this way
himself, and inspires others to do so, means that however much
we may want to criticise a good many of his views on philosophy,
we cannot but recognise that he is one of the great teachers and
leaders of our time.

of Marius did but follow the line taken by the majority of educated persons, though to a different issue.    Pitched to a really high and serious key, the precept Be perfect in regard to what is here and now: the precept of ' culture ' as it is called, or of a complete education—might at least save him from the vulgarity and heaviness of a generation, certainly of no general fineness of temper, though with a material well-being abundant enough.    Conceded that what is secure in our existence is but the sharp apex of the present moment between two hypothetical eternities, and all that is real in our experience but a series of fleeting impressions . . . then he at least, in whom those fleeting impressions—faces, voices, material sunshine—were very real and imperious, might well set himself to the consideration, how such actual moments as they passed might be made to yield their utmost, by the most dexterous training of capacity.    Amid abstract metaphysical doubts, as to what might lie one step only beyond that experience, reinforcing the deep, original materialism or earthliness of human nature itself, bound so intimately to the sensuous world, let him at least make the most of what was ' here and now.'    In the actual dimness of ways from means to ends—ends in themselves desirable, yet for the most part distant and for him, certainly, below the visible horizon—he would at all events be

sure that the means, to use the well-worn terminology, should have something of finality about
them, and themselves partake in a measure of the
more excellent nature of ends—that the means
should justify the end."

And with regard to the third attitude—the
Stoic detachment or indifference—we can only
recall the disquieting analogy of the Roman
Stoics. The evidence here points to the negative
and sterile character of a philosophy which has
lost the zest of life, and the feeling of the precious-
ness of the present, in spite of all its welter and
confusion; and to the fate of the chaos of the
present when it is left without any guidance from
philosophy. It looks as though philosophy becomes inert and negative—a mere being learned
in the ideas of others—if it fails to discover and
sympathise with whatever creative forces there
may be in contemporary life.

Therefore we should turn with gratitude to
Whitehead, if for nothing else, for his showing
us that it is possible to be at the same time both
a rationalist and a romantic. In the battles of
romantics and rationalists one is constantly conscious, on the one hand, of a vague emotion-
alism, and refusal to face facts; on the other hand,
of something negative and over-precious. But the
real thinker combines the contribution of both.
He knows, as Hegel did, that " nothing great

can be done without passion "; but he refuses to slip into the anti-intellectualism of the sentimental romantic. His quality of mind can be described in Sir Walter Raleigh's words about Wordsworth, as that of one " who faced the fact and against whom the fact did not prevail. To know him is to learn courage; to walk with him is to feel the visitings of a larger, purer air, and the peace of an unfathomable sky."

Whitehead's philosophy can hardly be described as an arid rationalism when a great part of the Philosophy of Organism is (as will be seen) based on the appreciation of feeling; and on notions drawn from æsthetics.[1]   Yet he is none the less a rationalist; but a rationalist who shows us that the emotions stirred by the intellectual beauty of reason, and indeed the intellectual love of God, are real emotions.   And he teaches us once more that the attitude of the true rationalist is one of penetrating sincerity; of speculative boldness; and of complete humility before fact and before the puny scope of the human mind when it tries " to sound the depths in the nature of things."[2]

[1] *Cf.* also *Science and the Modern World*, p. 281 : "The true rationalism must always transcend itself by recurrence to the concrete in search of inspiration.   A self-satisfied rationalism is in effect a form of anti-rationalism.   It means an arbitrary halt at a particular set of abstractions."

[2] *Process and Reality*, p. x ; *Concept of Nature*, p. 73 ; *Principles of Natural Knowledge*, p. viii.

# CHAPTER IV

## SOME PRIMARY NOTIONS OF THE PHILOSOPHY
## OF ORGANISM

An organism is the community of the Universe in the service of the individual.—C. G. STONE, *The Social Contract of the Universe.*

The great, the sacred law of partaking, the noiseless step of continuity . . . Whoso partakes of a thing enjoys his share, and comes in contact with the thing and its other partakers. But he claims no more. His share in no way negates the thing or their share ; nor does it preclude his possession of reserved and private powers with which they have nothing to do, and which are not all absorbed in the mere function of sharing. Why may not the world be a sort of republican banquet of this sort, where all the qualities of being respect one another's personal sacredness, yet sit at the common table ?—WILLIAM JAMES, *On Some Hegelisms.*

In this chapter I wish to draw attention to some of the dominant notions of the Philosophy of Organism. It may therefore be simply regarded as a series of notes on *Process and Reality*, I., ch. ii., the chapter in which Whitehead sets out his Categorical Scheme.

Before proceeding to this, we may note the way in which he uses the term " categories." He clearly does not mean what Kant means when he speaks of the categories as the moulds into which all possible experience is cast; nor what, for instance, Professor Alexander (with whom, in many ways, Whitehead has closer affinities than with any other modern philosopher) means, when he talks of categories as all-pervasive features of Space-Time. He is rather nearer, at any rate as regards his Categories of Existence, to the Aristotelian use of the word, to express the different ways in which things can be, or the different kinds into which reality can be classified.[1] The Categories of Explanation are more puzzling; they are expansions of the notion of an entity, *i.e.* really, of the Categories of Existence. As Whitehead himself says, there may be an indefinite number of them, so it is a little difficult to see why he should give just twenty-seven, and then state that any possible explanation of what is meant by being an actual entity should come under one of them. Nor are they by any means always mutually independent. The point of them, however, is that they do serve to expand the notion of an actual entity; they are the definitions by which the discussions and applications in the rest of the book must be guided. The Categorical Obligations are clearer—they are

[1] It is however difficult to see why prehensions, nexūs, propositions, multiplicities and contrasts should be described as " categories of existence." They are surely rather modes in which actual entities and eternal objects can be together.

conditions to which all possible experience must conform. But this does not mean that they are legislated by the mind. They are the permanent characteristics of actuality; and in this way, come near to Alexander's meaning of " categories."

Besides these more specific categories, Whitehead has a " Category of the Ultimate," which differs from the others in its complete generality, *i.e.* it underlies every type of existence whatsoever. That is to say, it is the final notion of the most complete generality to which, as we saw, a metaphysical system must come, and for which no further reason or explanation beyond itself can be given. Thus it might be said that it is the ultimate irrationality which must be accepted simply as " given "[1] and beyond which we cannot go. Whitehead holds that it is necessary for every metaphysic to come in the end to some ultimate irrationality. But this may simply mean that it is the furthest back that it has been able to push the process of rational explanation; and the trouble is that it has never really gone far enough back, so that it finds its " Category of the Ultimate " somewhere short of complete generality. The example in older metaphysics is of course the concept of Substance;

[1] For the notion of " givenness " in this sense, *cf.* A. E. Taylor, *Plato, the Man and His Work*, 3rd edition (London, 1929), p. 455.

5

in Alexander's metaphysic it is Space-Time. Whitehead defines it as Creativity, by which he explains he means the bare general notion of the possibility of there being anything at all— what is involved in the notion of " any " or " the." This he finds to involve the notions of " one " and of " many "—not the more special mathematical notion of the number one, but the bare idea of singularity, along with the bare idea of disjunctive diversity. This notion—that the fundamental thing that can be said about the universe is that it is One and Many—is of course a very old one. But note, One *and* Many, not One or Many. The puzzle was set by the Greek metaphysicians; yet almost every metaphysic ends as a pluralism or a monism and fails to do justice to the other side. But the Philosophy of Organism is another attempt to do justice to both. It is an analysis of how " in their natures, entities are disjunctively ' many ' in process of passage into conjunctive unity ";[1] of how " the universe is at once the multiplicity of *res veræ* and the solidarity of *res veræ*."[2]

Creativity, then, is the notion of pure activity underlying the nature of things. And the most

[1] *Process and Reality*, p. 29 (32).

[2] *Ibid.,* p. 234 (254). For Whitehead's use of the term *res vera* see also p. viii. He claims to be using it in the Cartesian sense, of an individual real fact, with all its attributes and accidents about it.

general thing that can be said about it is that
it is the urge towards differentiation and unification, *i.e.* towards the individuation of itself into
many actualities, which are called its " creatures,"
and towards the growing together of these
creatures into new unities. Creativity itself is
simply pure, formless activity; and it is uncharac-
terised, telling by itself no tale of the creatures
which may characterise it. As therefore combining both the notions of pure potentiality and
of the principle of individuation, it answers to the
Aristotelian Primary Matter (ὕλη).

There will be a good deal more to say about
Creativity, and its characterisation by its own
creatures, when we come to examine the notion
of " God." We can only repeat in passing that
the Philosophy of Organism is an attempt to
describe the way in which each new characterisation of creativity exhibits both the unity and the
plurality of the universe. It is a new creature,
adding to the disjunctive diversity of the world;
but by its objectifying of its feelings of the rest
of the world into its own process of self-
formation, it is a new unification of the world,
a new way in which the universe becomes one.
The process of creation is therefore rhythmic
(as Empedocles forecast, in his description of
a primordial Love and Strife); and it is the eternal

process of the breaking up of the One into the Many and the growing together again, in a new kind of unity of the Many into One. This has a Hegelian ring about it; but, as will be seen, with a difference.

The name, "The Philosophy of Organism," has another implication which brings out one of the fundamental convictions underlying it. This is that it is concerned exclusively with "the becoming, the being, and the relatedness of actual entities"; with a relatedness which always "has its foundation in the relatedness of actualities," and is "wholly concerned with the appropriation of the dead by the living."[1] This means that it is essentially an attempt to exhibit fact as something concrete. It is a protest against the tendency in science and philosophy to look on abstractions as anything more than abstractions, *i.e.* as capable of existing, though they can be thought of, separately in their own right. This he calls, in a phrase which has now become famous, "The Fallacy of Misplaced Concreteness."[2] This fallacy has led philosophers to talk of sensation, awareness, and so on, as if they were anything more than the activities of concrete actualities. Philosophy therefore imposes all sorts of difficulties on itself by starting from abstract universals, and

[1] *Process and Reality*, pp. viii (ix).
[2] *Science and the Modern World*, p. 72.

then asking how concrete fact can be built up of them; or by starting from an "intuition" of individual concrete fact, and then being unable to say how it can exemplify universals. Instead the problem should be stated as: How can concrete fact exhibit characteristics, which can be considered as abstract from itself, and described in some kind of symbolism? Therefore, to put this in Whitehead's own words, "Philosophy is explanatory of abstraction and not of concreteness. It is by reason of their instinctive grasp of this ultimate truth that, in spite of much association with arbitrary fancifulness and atavistic mysticism, types of Platonic philosophy retain their abiding appeal; *they seek the forms in the facts*."[1]

That is to say, concrete individual fact achieves definiteness, *i.e.* is characterised, only by exhibiting forms which can be exhibited by different particulars, at different times. As Whitehead puts this, fancifully, in *Science and the Modern World*,[2] a colour "haunts time like a spirit"— it comes and it goes. The form "red" is no reason why there should be this particular red thing; yet the definiteness of a fact is due to the forms which "participate" in it, while the concrete fact is always more than the sum of its forms. This notion will be further dis-

[1] *Process and Reality*, p. 27 (30).
[2] P. 121.

cussed in the following chapter on the eternal objects.

We must pass now to three other notions, which Whitehead singles out in ch. ii., § 1, as fundamental, and as showing " an endeavour to base philosophical thought upon the most concrete elements in our experience." These are the notions of an " actual entity," a " prehension," and the " Ontological Principle."

An actual entity or an actual occasion is one of the final real things of which the universe is made up. Without prejudicing the question what these final real things are, or what this final real thing is, we can say confidently that our fundamental intuitions of Nature show it to us as a going-on, or happening of something. In physical science we are trying to discern interconnections and regularities in this " something which is going on," or " passage " as it is well called in *The Concept of Nature*; and in metaphysics we are seeking to exhibit what we know of its general character. If then we say that this which is going on must be something, and not merely nonentity, we can go on to say that the " laws," or permanent characters that it exhibits are the result of its being what it is. The fundamental question is, therefore, what is the nature of the actual entity or actual entities in which this " passage " consists ? We have just said that our intuition of Nature makes us

feel that it is a *process*—something is going on
—we talk of " Time like an ever-rolling stream "
and so forth.

οἵη περ φύλλων γενεή, τοίη δὲ καὶ ἀνδρῶν.
φύλλα τὰ μὲν τ' ἄνεμος χαμάδις χέει, ἄλλα δε θ' ὕλη
τηλεθόωσα φύει, ἔαρος δ' ἐπιγίγνεται ὥρῃ·
ὡς ἀνδρῶν γενεὴ ἡ μὲν φύει, ἡ δ' ἀπολήγει.[1]

Yet what if this deep, primitive intuition of the
passage of Nature is an illusion ?   What if the
final real things are permanent, eternal, and
change and process is simply an apparent unfolding
of them in time; or the transitoriness of some of
their merely trivial and unessential qualities ?
Such on the whole has been the conclusion of most
of the older philosophies.   The final facts are
then a bundle of attributes and accidents, held
together by a *vinculum substantiale*, itself unchangeable (or changeable only by a miracle,
as in the Mass), and in the last resort, like
Locke's substance, a " something I know not
what," in which qualities inhere.   This of course
would not be true without reservations of all
doctrines of substance.   Aristotelian and mediæval philosophy showed determined attempts to
grapple with the problems of becoming and
individuation.   But on the whole it is fair to say
that the result of this kind of view has been

[1] *Iliad*, vi., 146 *sq.*

either a monadology, which looks on individual substances as absolutely distinct, and self-contained, with the attributes which they support; or a monism which, by allowing for internal relations and organic interconnection, ends by swallowing up the individuals, and leaving them only an adjectival existence in the one substance.

The Philosophy of Organism, on the other hand, starts by accepting the intuition of the passage of Nature. It therefore sets out to take the idea of Process seriously. So Whitehead, in common with other modern philosophers, especially those who have been influenced by the new physics, has called the ultimate facts of nature " events "; and bids us look on nature as a complex of events. Beyond events there is to be nothing—no space and time, no matter, no " laws of nature," no material substance like the ether in which they can take place. " The material called ether is merely the outcome of a metaphysical craving. The continuity of nature is the continuity of events."[1] Russell aptly remarks[2] that the ether seemed to be such a convenient and comfortable thing to believe in because its properties were merely those demanded by its functions. " In fact, like a painfully good boy, it only did what it was told, and might

[1] *Principles of Natural Knowledge*, 6. 3.
[2] *Analysis of Matter*, p. 20.

therefore be expected to die young." Whitehead says, however, that we might still speak of an " ether of events " to express the assumption "that something is going on everywhere and always."

But the original, and perhaps most important feature of Whitehead's treatment of nature as a network of events is his view that the property of events is to extend over other events, so that the large-scale events are systems of atomic events, which are those which, in *Process and Reality*, are called actual entities, or actual occasions.[1] The interconnections between events, including what we call spatial and temporal relations, can therefore be reduced to types of this fundamental relation of " extensive connection."[2] This is an extremely important idea; and it will be taken up and discussed more fully in Chapter VI.

Beyond these final atomic events, or actual entities, there is therefore nothing. The Philosophy of Organism is concerned solely with "the becoming, the being, and the relatedness of actual entities." Everything that can be said about the universe must be said about an actual entity, or group or nexus of actual entities. They

[1] This is clearly pointed out in the review of *Process and Reality* in the *Journal of Philosophical Studies*, January, 1931.

[2] Cf. *Principles of Natural Knowledge, passim,* but especially 1. 5 ; *Concept of Nature,* pp. 58 *sq.* ; *Process and Reality,* Pt. IV., The Theory of Extension.

5*

may differ in richness, or degree, of quality; but the categorical principles they exemplify must be the same.  If our metaphysical scheme were correct, these would be the principles there formulated.  God is an actual entity; and so is the most trivial puff of existence.[1]  Whitehead here states summarily his view of the ultimate nature of all actual entities; they are " drops of experience," that is, events in the process of becoming, with their own subjective immediacy. This naturally reminds us of Bradley's insistence that " to be real is to be indissolubly one thing with sentience . . .  Being and reality are in brief one thing with sentience; they can neither be opposed to, not even in the end distinguished from it."[2]  Whitehead's view does not of course necessarily imply that there is in the end a single and all-inclusive experience; nor (any more than Bradley's) that sentient experience need be conscious.  But both views are equally a repudiation of what he calls " vacuous actuality," that is to say, actuality devoid of subjective experience in *any* form; the notion that an " essence," or a mathematical formula, or " law " can have any sort of existence apart from concrete fact, which, as actual, is always in some measure a process of becoming or experiencing.

[1] *Process and Reality*, p. 24 (28).
[2] *Appearance and Reality*, p. 146.

This brings us to what Whitehead calls his "Ontological Principle." Here he is using a term in a sense which is etymologically correct, but different from its familiar use. The Ontological Principle is a statement that since everything whatsoever that can be called real must be an actual entity, or complex of actual entities, therefore anything which can be said about anything, any reasons, or descriptions, must be due to actual entities and their characteristics. The reason for everything which happens must be sought in the nature of actual entities. This is a sort of detective story view of the universe—we have not found out the sufficient reason for anything, until we have tracked it down to some actual entity or entities. This sounds obvious common sense, so it is worth pointing out that it is counter to a good deal of modern philosophy.

(a) It is a direct challenge to the doctrine of Subsistence of the Critical Realists; the view that essences which do not exist "subsist," so that they are available for repeated exemplification in matters of fact.[1] Whitehead looks on this as really a fudge—a suggestion that something can

[1] For the connection of this notion of essences with that of another "vacuous actuality," as a substratum in which they must inhere to become actualised, see an article, "The Concrete Universal," by M. B. Foster in *Mind*, January, 1931, in which he argues that "Substance is the nemesis of essence."

float out of nothing. Essences, or universals, as "forms of definiteness" cannot merely float,[1] detached from any form of existence. They must be grounded somehow in the nature of existence, that is to say, of some actual entity. How Whitehead conceives this to be we shall try to show in the next chapter.

(*b*) It is also a challenge to the view of the New Realists, who tend to make mind into a "vacuous actuality," by describing it as mere apprehension —the place from which something is observed, without this involving any subjective activity on the part of the observer.

(*c*) It runs counter to a more subtle tendency in modern philosophy, namely that of looking for a sufficient reason for a thing in a mathematical formula, and thinking that when we are left with the formula, we have something ultimate. Whitehead on the other hand is protesting that there is nothing finally actual about a formula, apart from some kind of sentient experience. He has here been accused of a British obstinacy like that of Lord Kelvin, who, it will be remembered, said he could be content with no piece of mathematical reasoning unless he could construct a model; as contrasted with the more abstract continental thinkers who could be perfectly

---

[1] Here again, a recollection of Bradley's insistence that there are no " floating adjectives " is obvious.

content simply with formulæ. This accusation
seems a strange one to make against a pure mathematician; and those who make it must feel that
he is going back on his earlier view that logical
constructions are always to be preferred to
inferred entities.[1] Russell has argued that in
physics, and also in philosophy, a constructed
function, which should where possible be expressed in mathematical symbolism, should be
sought instead of an actual entity, when we are
seeking "explanations," which are simply in
fact correlations of such functions. This is
applying Occam's razor, "entia non multipli-
canda præter necessitatem," to cutting out
Existence altogether as an ultimate philosophical
notion, except as saying there is a value satisfying
a function. Whitehead's Philosophy of Organism
is now throughout an insistence that Existence
*is* a fundamental notion of metaphysics, since he
holds that, though things may exhibit qualities
which can be described as mathematical forms,
these forms are only arrived at by abstraction,
and cannot be real, or, it appears, he now holds
even possible, apart from a relation to existence
—*i.e.* actuality invested with some form of
subjective experience. We may say that if this
seems to represent a departure from earlier views,
it is because he is turning from the attitude

[1] *Cf.* Russell, *Mysticism and Logic*, pp. 155 *sq.*

of the logician to that of the metaphysician. Russell has said[1] that as a mathematical logician he is not called upon to assert whether, for instance, classes exist as real entities or not. Existence is not a fundamental logical notion, *i.e.* it is not an analytic concept.[2] No logical principle can assert existence except under a hypothesis, *i.e.* we cannot have the complete assertion that a propositional function $\phi x$ is sometimes true, but can only say that *if* $\phi x$ is sometimes true, arguments satisfying it exist; or that there is a term $c$ such that $\phi x$ is always equivalent to " $x$ is $c$." For instance, " The author of Waverley exists " means,

(*i.*) " $x$ wrote Waverley " is not always false.
(*ii.*) " If $x$ and $y$ wrote Waverley, $x$ and $y$ are identical " is always true.

When however we pass from logic to metaphysics, Whitehead's Ontological Principle claims that we cannot be content with this merely

[1] *Introduction to Mathematical Philosophy* (London, 1919), pp. 183-184.

[2] The logical meaning of " existence " is defined in *Principia Mathematica*, 2nd edition (Cambridge, 1925), vol. i., 14.02 (p. 174) ; and again by Russell, *Introduction to Mathematical Philosophy*, pp. 164, 177-179. It is said that it can only be significantly asserted of descriptions, not of names. What we usually consider as names, such as Homer or Scott, are seen on analysis to be really descriptions.

hypothetical assertion; or rather that metaphysics must make the final assumption that "something given exists." But as far as logic and pure mathematics go, he would allow that the existence of real entities corresponding to their conventional definitions may remain purely hypothetical. Yet even when he wrote his *Treatise on Universal Algebra*, he argued that for a mathematical science of any importance to be founded on conventional definitions "the entities created by them must have properties which bear some affinity to the properties of existing things."[1]

The full significance of the Ontological Prin-

---

[1] *A Treatise on Universal Algebra* (Cambridge, 1898), pp. vi, vii. The whole paragraph from which this sentence is taken is worth quoting in connection with the distinction under discussion. " Mathematical reasoning is deductive in the sense that it is based upon definitions which, as far as the validity of the reasoning is concerned (apart from any existential import), need only the test of self-consistency. Thus no external verification of definitions is required in mathematics as long as it is considered merely as mathematics. . . . Mathematical definitions either possess an existential import or are conventional. A mathematical definition with an existential import is the result of an act of pure abstraction. Such definitions are the starting points of applied mathematical sciences. . . . In order that a mathematical science of any importance may be founded upon conventional definitions the entities created by them must have properties which bear some affinity to the properties of existing things. . . . The existential import of a mathematical definition attaches to it, if at all, *qua* mixed mathematics : *qua* pure mathematics, ·mathematical definitions must be conventional."

ciple comes out when we consider what meaning we are to ascribe to the "laws of nature." This will be taken up in Chapter VII., in connection with the Concept of Order. The kind of view we are to expect is summarised in the 18th Category of Explanation, which is really a statement of the Ontological Principle. Any "conditions" to which the process of becoming of any actual entity conforms are determined either by its own "real internal constitution," or by that of other actual entities in its world. Thus the conditions known as the laws of nature are not mechanical or logical laws considered as abstractions. They are descriptions of the characters of the "real internal constitutions" of actual entities—of the actual entity called "God," or of wide societies of other actual entities. Whitehead quotes the passage from Locke (*Essay*, III., iii., 15) from which the phrase "real internal constitution" is drawn. It is one of those inspired phrases with which Locke has enriched philosophy. The "real essence" of a thing, is here suggested to be synonymous with its constitution or structure. Its use in the Philosophy of Organism may also be compared with the Aristotelian doctrine of the form as the organisation of a certain structure to serve a certain end. The 23rd Category of Explanation means that the structure of an actual entity is the way in which it organises itself in

order to become itself.[1] This is elucidated
further by the notion of the " Subjective Aim "
(to which we shall return presently).

We come next to the notion of a prehension.
This is a happy term, since it expresses the relation of an actual entity to other actual entities
in a word which involves neither conscious awareness (as would apprehension), nor a merely static
and mechanical link.   " Prehension " means the
grasping by one actual entity of some aspect or
part of other actual entities, and appropriating
them in the formation of its own nature.[2]   How
this is to be conceived will be seen further in
Chapter VI., when we come to the Theory of
Feelings.   It must be sufficient here just to note
this general meaning of " prehension," and to
refer the reader to *Science and the Modern World*
(chapter iv.) for a full and clear statement of it.
Actual entities are there described as " prehensive
occasions," that is to say, events or concrete
facts of becoming, which arise out of their interrelations with other events throughout nature.
A " thing," therefore, is, broadly speaking, a

---

[1] *Cf.* J. S. Haldane, *The Sciences and Philosophy* (London,
1929), pp. 326 *sq.*, where structure is described as the expression
of a co-ordinated persistence of activity.

[2] Or, in the language of *Science and the Modern World*
(pp. 98 *sq.*), " a unification of perspectives from a standpoint
here."

creative synthesis of its relations to other events, or rather a centre of experiencing (*feeling*) which is characterised by the way in which it feels other events.  Each actual entity is a new fact, because it is a new centre of experience, or act of feeling; but it is what it is also because of the nature of other events, which it feels.  This, it will be foreseen, is the line along which the Philosophy of Organism will try to combine the notions of atomism and relativity; or pluralism and the view of nature as an organic unity.  Nature is to be looked on as an interwoven network of events, every event, by being what it is, conditioning all the others.  We may refer to a statement of this, as a general statement of the " principle of relativity " in the 4th Category of Explanation.  It is there said that " it belongs to the nature of a being that it is a potential for every becoming."  This recalls the definition of Being in *Sophist* 247*e* as the capacity of acting or being acted upon.  That is to say that everything either does or may enter into the being of everything else; you cannot get behind the influence of things upon each other.  So you cannot abstract an entity from its context of the whole world.

But at the same time this again avoids turning into the extreme Monism of Hegelian types of organic philosophy by taking seriously the idea

of Process.[1]  In Hegelian organic philosophy
the notion of universal internal relation is taken
to mean that the One becomes only apparently
Many.  Whitehead's Philosophy of Organism,
on the other hand, describes how the Many arise
atomically, as new events, but are characterised
by the way in which they feel all the rest.  So
each entity forms a new and unique synthesis of its
relations to the whole of the rest of the world, so
that it becomes the whole seen from a new centre.
We may recall Leibniz' monad mirroring the
whole universe from its point of view.  But we
have here a process of an active growing out,
instead of simply reflecting or perceiving, of the
rest of its world.  Actual entities arise out of
their prehensions of each other; this secures the
solidarity of the order of nature.  But they have
also their private and unique side, since each
organises its prehensions of the rest of the world
into the forming of its own " real internal constitution " in its peculiar way.  We can here see
clearly the distinction between this and Bradley's
view of experience, to which Whitehead nevertheless acknowledges a considerable debt.[2]  They
agree in making experience or sentience fundamental.  But whereas Bradley speaks of experi-

---

[1] " Nature," he says (*Science and the Modern World*, p. 104),
is " the locus of organisms in process of development."

[2] *Process and Reality*, p. vii (viii).

ence as essentially one and all-inclusive, and only apparently differentiated into many, Whitehead looks on each act of feeling as a new act, and therefore each new way of experiencing the world as adding a new experience to it.[1]

Hence the importance of what he variously calls the final causation or Subjective Aim of an actual entity; and why he repeatedly says that no pluralistic philosophy can be made to work apart from the notion of final causation. He uses this not in the Aristotelian sense of a fixed end determining a thing's growth, but rather to describe what has been called an "end in view," *i.e.* a teleology immanent in the actual occasion, which organises the data presented to it by the other occasions, which constitute the rest of its world, in the accomplishing of its own process of self-formation. So he often speaks of an actual occasion as a "concrescence," that is, a growing together of many things into a new unity.[2] Professor Lloyd Morgan, in a paper called "Subjective Aim in Whitehead's Philosophy,"[3] has taken exception to the language Whitehead is using here. He protests against his application of terms such as "subjective aim," "satisfaction," "mental and physical

[1] *Ibid.*, p. 234 (254).

[2] Cf. *Process and Reality*, p. 56 (65), where it is stated that the essence of an actual entity consists solely in the fact that it is a prehending thing.

[3] *Journal of Philosophical Studies*, July, 1931.

prehensions " to " sub-living organisms," without having said that they are to be divested of all their usual psychological meaning. Whitehead has, however, certainly said often enough that these terms must not be understood as necessarily implying conscious behaviour. But the real crux in justifying his use of them lies in whether Professor Lloyd Morgan is right in maintaining that " Teleological relatedness is a very late outcome of a long process of actual concrescence "; or whether these terms describe something to be found in some measure all down the scale of existence. We may recall the remarkable passage from Bacon, quoted in *Science and the Modern World* (p. 58): " It is certain that all bodies whatsoever, though they have no sense, yet they have perception; for when one body is applied to another, there is a kind of election to embrace that which is agreeable, and to exclude or expel that which is ingrate; and whether the body be alterant or altered, evermore a perception precedeth operation; for else all bodies would be alike one to another." (κ.τ.λ.)

On the alternative view, it is necessary to draw a line between mechanical and organic nature, and this is becoming increasingly difficult. An independent support for Whitehead's view is found in Professor J. S. Haldane's Gifford Lectures[1]

[1] *The Sciences and Philosophy.*

where he argues that neither mechanism nor vitalism is any longer an adequate theory; that we find everywhere co-ordinated activity.   Biologists are certainly recognising that the organisation of structure is the central theoretical problem of their science;[1] but probably few (and I doubt whether Professor Haldane would be one of them) would yet go so far as Whitehead in saying that " Biology is the study of the larger organisms, whereas Physics is the study of the smaller organisms."[2]   We can, however, only note here that Whitehead is certainly committing himself to the view that teleological structure, in the sense of co-ordinated persistence of activity, is fundamental in every kind of actuality; and recognise that, if the language in which he describes this seems strange and anthropomorphic, yet modern philosophers still seem fairly divided on whether or no " unconscious purpose " is really a contradiction in terms.[3]   He therefore

[1] *Cf.* J. H. Woodger, *Biological Principles*, Pt. II., ch. iii., especially pp. 174 *sq.*

[2] *Science and the Modern World*, p. 145.   Contrast Haldane, *The Sciences and Philosophy*, p. 326.

[3] Woodger (*op. cit.*, p. 432) makes a distinction between the word " purpose," which he restricts to conscious human purpose, and the general term " teleology," for which he quotes the following definition by L. T. Hobhouse : (1) A process in time with some definite result ; (2) an element of value in the result ; (3) this element to be a determining factor in the process by which it is brought about.

calls every type of relation between actualities a prehension of some kind. This holds of the types of relation known as perception, or awareness, as well as those more naturally described as feeling. It should be noted that this theory of feeling does not necessarily demand contiguity of actual entities in space and time. It simply expresses the general assumption of the Philosophy of Organism that one actual entity affects, and so enters into the being, or " objectifies " itself in another. In fact it will be seen that space and time are among the most systematic relations between actual entities. The evidence from physical science at present suggests that physical prehensions are negligible except for contiguous, or mediately contiguous occasions; but " action at a distance " is still even here an open question; and in the case of mental prehensions there would seem to be some support for its possibility in the evidences for telepathy.[1] By the " objectification " of one entity in another is meant its contribution to the process of the becoming of another which feels it.[2] Since an actual entity arises by objectifying aspects of other actual entities in its own nature, it has an immediate feeling of every part of its own subjective experience as involving other actual entities.

Every prehension has therefore what is here

[1] Cf. *Process and Reality*, p. 436 (469).
[2] Category of Explanation xxiv.

called a "vector" character; that is to say it shows the total experience as involving at least two terms; importing the term "vector," from mathematical physics where it means a directed magnitude, involving determinate direction from one term to another—*e.g.* the origin O to P.

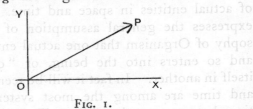

Fig. 1.

Hence, as will be seen more clearly in the discussion of Perception, feeling of an external world as causally affecting us is prior to conscious awareness of it as an object of perception. Moreover the emotion in which the subject's drive towards its own self-formation consists is felt as derived from objects and directed towards them. Thus the subject-object relation is understood in a wider and more primitive sense than when it is restricted to the relations of knowing and perceiving. Every actual entity emerges from the background of the world which it feels, and its own nature might be described as the way in which it organises its perspectives of the rest of the world.[1] These *ways in which* actual entities

[1] There is an interesting analysis of this with particular regard to the theory of perception, and of mind as arising from

unify their prehensions in their process of self-formation are called subjective forms. Some of the kinds of subjective form are enumerated in Category of Explanation xiii., as emotions, valuations, purposes, adversions, aversions, consciousness.

As the intensity of the subjective experience of an actual entity grows, it becomes highly selective of the totality of the world out of which it arises. This is because the notions of prehension and of subjective form are complementary. Each actuality prehends in some form the whole of its world; but the way in which it prehends, and hence the degree of emphasis or negligible importance of its prehension of another entity will depend on its own subjective form. We thus see (*a*) that all prehension involves abstraction, since it is the raising into relief of some aspects of the thing prehended and the ignoring of others; and (*b*) that what aspects of one entity will be prehended by another will depend on their " relevance " to its subjective form. So though every entity can potentially enter into the concrescence of every other, the mode in which it actually enters is conditioned by the subjective form of the other.[1]

the organising of perspectives of the rest of the world in a paper by Professor G. H. Mead of the University of Chicago in the Proceedings of the 6th International Congress of Philosophy. See also *Science and the Modern World*, pp. 92 *sq.*

[1] Category of Explanation vi.

This notion of " relevance " is an extremely important one for the Philosophy of Organism. We shall notice it again in connection with the eternal objects. By using it to show how an actual entity raises into relief certain of its prehensions, and dismisses the contribution of others to its subjective aim as trivial or negligible or incompatible, it will attempt to combine a view of organic interconnection with a view of the essential and unessential relations of an actual entity, and so defend the possibility of finite true propositions about it. We should also note here the distinction between positive and negative prehensions.[1]   A positive prehension is a " feeling " —an admission by the actual entity of some element of others as affecting its own process of becoming. All other actual entities are prehended positively in some measure, though in infinitely varying degrees of emphasis. A negative prehension is said to eliminate from feeling. It is a rejected alternative—a dismissal by an actual entity of something as incompatible with its subjective aim. Negative prehensions hold only of prehensions of eternal objects.[2] Something which is red negatively prehends blue, by excluding it as an alternative possibility. Whitehead

[1] Category of Explanation xii.

[2] An analysis of this notion, as well as a discussion of what Whitehead means by the eternal objects, will be found in the next chapter.

has to maintain that such a relation of exclusion is a bond of a certain kind (since the reason for it is to be found in the nature of the actual entity and the eternal object considered together), if he is to maintain the universal relativity of everything to everything else. At the same time, by the notions of relevance and incompatibility he tries to avoid the difficulties of an out and out monism.

When we seek to analyse or describe an actual entity we are considering some of its prehensions, positive or negative, of other actual entities and eternal objects. These prehensions all contribute their element of definiteness to the total character of the actual entity; and in analysis, we are distinguishing some of these elements and considering them in abstraction. But this division of an actual entity into its prehensions loses the final causation—the subjective aim—which is making this concrescence of prehensions into a real (*concrete*) unity. Note that this is just what happens in scientific analysis. The element of final causation by which an entity constitutes itself is lost. This does not mean that scientific analysis into prehensions is false. It does give us an analysis of the morphology, or pattern, formed by the prehensions of an actual entity, which describes certain real features of its definite character, but omits the " real internal constitution " on which in the last re-

sort these depend. So two descriptions of an
actual entity are necessary;[1] one, that of scientific
analysis, which describes the prehensions of actual
entities in a nexus, as " public matters of fact ";
the other, the feeling from the inside of the subjective aim, which is a " private matter of fact,"
which, Whitehead says, can only be got by a
Bergsonian intuition. These two sides are both
necessary for the complete description of anything.
But it is pointed out[2] that they are not entirely
independent, since *how* an actual entity becomes
constitutes *what* it is. This follows from Category
of Explanation vi.—the statement that the mode
in which an actual entity prehends its world
depends on its subjective aim. But this again
involves taking seriously the idea of Process. The
actual entity is not something with a character
from which its feelings result. What it is arises
out of the way in which it feels.

Scientific analysis in terms of prehensions is
called " division."[3] The exhibiting of a connection between prehensions is called " Co-ordinate Division."[4] This " co-ordination of prehensions expresses the publicity of the world, so far
as it can be considered in abstraction from private

[1] Category of Explanation viii.
[2] Category of Explanation ix.
[3] Category of Explanation x.
[4] See *Process and Reality*, Pt. IV.

genesis. Prehensions have public careers, but they are born privately."[1]

This explains why, on this view, the analysis of an actual entity in terms of the static morphology of its prehensions does not distort its nature in the way in which Bergson claims. It is because when an actual entity has become, or in Whitehead's phrase, has "achieved definiteness," it is fully coherent, a unity in which each element plays its own part as contributing to the total, and no element is duplicated. This final stage is called the "satisfaction."[2] Analysis of the morphology of prehensions is analysis of the different elements which have brought each its unique contribution to the "satisfaction" (or perhaps we may say equilibrium) which is the completed actuality. We may illustrate this by thinking of a picture, or a play, in which the significance of any one element can be seen when the whole is completed.[3]

For this general view of the essence of a thing as consisting of its prehensions *plus* its "real internal constitution," Whitehead refers us to two other inspired passages in Locke; the one[4] where Locke says that *powers* form a great part of our complex ideas of substances; that is to say, the

[1] *Op. cit.* p. 411 (444).

[2] Categories of Explanation xxv., xxvi.

[3] This notion will be discussed more fully at the beginning of Chapter VII.    [4] *Essay* II., xxiii., 7 and 10.

capacities of things for acting and being acted upon in certain ways under certain conditions make up our ideas of their nature; and the other, a passage[1] in which Locke forecasts the main doctrine of the Philosophy of Organism. " For we are wont to consider the substances we meet with, each of them as an entire thing by itself, having all its qualities in itself, and independent of other things. . . . We are then quite out of the way, when we think that things contain within themselves the qualities that appear to us in them; and we in vain search for that constitution within the body of a fly or an elephant, upon which depend those qualities and powers we observe in them. For which perhaps to understand them aright, we ought to look not only beyond this our earth and atmosphere, but beyond the sun or remotest star our eyes have discovered. . . . This is certain, things, however absolute and entire they seem in themselves, are but retainers to other parts of nature for that which they are most taken notice of by us. Their observable qualities, actions and powers are owing to something without them; and there is not so complete and perfect a part that we know of nature, which does not owe the being it has, and the excellencies of it, to its neighbours."

To substantiate his claim that the spirit of Philosophy of Organism is essentially Car-

[1] *Essay* IV., vi., 11.

tesian, rather than Kantian, Whitehead takes every opportunity such as this of pointing out analogies between his views and those of the philosophers from Descartes to Hume. Incidentally this means that he lets fall many extremely valuable *obiter dicta*, especially concerning Locke and Hume. These cannot all be taken uncritically, but they are often extremely suggestive and enlightening. They also perhaps help us to see what aspects of the philosophy of the seventeenth and eighteenth centuries are likely to be of permanent value, and what are of simply historical interest.

I have tried to point out and summarise in this chapter some of the leading notions of the Philosophy of Organism: creativity, actual entity, the Ontological Principle, prehension, subjective aim, objectification, satisfaction. These will all be taken up again in Chapters VI. and VII., in discussing the types of order of actual entities. I shall try in those chapters to deal more precisely with the concept of the process of becoming of actual entities through their prehensions of each other, and in so doing shall be taking note of the nine Categorical Obligations of the scheme; and also of the conception of nexūs, and of other kinds of societies of actual entities. The next chapter will be concerned with the nature of the eternal objects, or order of potentialities.

# CHAPTER V

## ARE THE ETERNAL OBJECTS PLATONIC IDEAS ?

a Power
That is the visible quality and shape
And image of right reason. . . .
Holds up before the mind intoxicate
With present objects, and the busy dance
Of things that pass away, a temperate show
Of objects that endure.

WORDSWORTH, *The Prelude.*

THE appearance of *Process and Reality* both provides us at last with the detailed formulation of the metaphysical scheme underlying Whitehead's earlier work and confirms a strong suspicion that the best general description that may be given of his philosophy is to say that it is a modern form of Platonism. Whitehead himself owns and welcomes this analogy,[1] but this suggestion of a possible way of interpreting him has not, so far as I am aware, been very much taken up. The aim of this chapter is therefore to trace some of what may be called " Platonic elements " in Whitehead's philosophy, considering it as a general metaphysical position, and in particular to ask whether

[1] *Process and Reality*, p. 54 (63).

his eternal objects can be looked on as in any way analogous to the Platonic Ideas.

"Platonism" is of course a term to be used advisedly. But one may perhaps guard oneself at the outset by distinguishing two ways in which it may be used. (*a*) It may refer to what, broadly speaking, we may call Platonic Studies, *i.e.* the specific, critical examination and elucidation of meanings in Plato's own philosophy. (*b*) It may stand for the general type of world view which has come to be considered as the Platonic tradition all through the history of thought. In this sense it may be used of the " Christian Platonists," from the Alexandrian Fathers, and St. Augustine, to the Cambridge Platonists, and finally to Dean Inge; of Wordsworth, and Emerson, and any others who have carried out an imaginative development of a line of thought suggested to them by reading Plato. The difficulty in this broader and looser use of the term " Platonism " is, of course, that it may lead us to read into Plato himself all sorts of ideas which are not really there—to the despair or annoyance of Platonic scholars in the former sense.

In speaking of " Platonism " in Whitehead's philosophy, I shall be using the term in the second sense; and at the outset, I shall take the precaution of pointing out that my aim is to suggest an interpretation of Whitehead rather than

6

of Plato.    I wish to try and show how certain
general ideas suggested by Plato are worked out
in a new form by Whitehead.

We cannot remind ourselves too often that we
must guard against the temptation of reading
modern ideas into Plato.    But when we turn
back to him after reading modern philosophy, we
are impressed by the way in which the general
questions he raised remain for us, as for him.
His answers, and the setting in which they are
given, may be in terms of very different categories
of thought from those of the modern world.    But
essentially he seems much nearer to us than much
modern philosophy, certainly than much of that
of the recent past.

With these preliminary reflections, let us now
turn to look at the view of Whitehead and that
of Plato considered as a general metaphysical
position.    Whitehead sees the general metaphysical problem, as Plato did, as the search
for " the forms in the facts,"[1] that is, as the
disentangling of the permanent elements in the
universe from the passing flux.    The immediate
sense of the flux of things—πάντα ῥεῖ—is, he
tells us,[2] the first and obvious delivery of uncritical thinking; and yet at the same time we
find in our moral and intellectual experience an

[1] *Op. cit.*, pp. 27 (30), 54 (63).
[2] *Ibid.*, p. 295 (317).

insistent demand for some permanence amid the flux. Therefore the problem of metaphysics is to find the right relation between the permanent, or timeless, and the changing elements in the universe, so as to do full justice to both.

Plato, in the same way, arrived at his Theory of Ideas from a desire to escape from the materialist, relativist metaphysics of the flux philosophers, the Heracleitean doctrines taught him by Cratylus. He insisted that such a view did not do justice to intellectual knowledge and moral experience. (In this latter point, at any rate, he was probably following Socrates.) So he was faced with the problem of the order amid change. How can Process exhibit structure and permanences ? His answer was that this is only possible because it " participates " in the forms. He seems to have arrived at this answer by arguing that knowledge can only be of what is permanent and does not change; so the object of abstract, conceptual thought is given a transcendent reality, and in contrast to it, the process, or flux, of things is given a merely derivative and deficient reality.

Whitehead,[1] on the other hand, starts with an analysis of the concept of Nature implied by physical science. He shows what a thorough overhauling of its basic notions modern physical

[1] In *The Concept of Nature, The Principles of Natural Knowledge*, and *The Principle of Relativity*.

science must undergo if it is to be truly "metaphysical." Nature can no longer be regarded as permanent "bits of matter" in space-time, but as an interrelated network of events, which come into being and perish.

Then how can the passing flux of events exhibit permanences ? Here Whitehead's answer is substantially the same as Plato's. It is through the "ingression" of "eternal objects." These eternal objects are forms of definiteness, "hows" for the process of becoming, which can only acquire determination by participating in them.

This general line of thought is a familiar one, and certainly Platonic. But before discussing it in more detail, it may be as well to remind ourselves of the fundamental problem to which it gives rise.

What is the status of the eternal objects ? This is of course but one form of the time-old problem as to the status of universals. It would seem as though there were three possible solutions open to Whitehead:

(a) Some form of Platonic realism. The forms are transcendent and timeless, existing *ante res*. (Plato, it will be remembered, while he took this view, left the locus of his realm of forms, and its exact relation to the world of becoming largely undefined, beyond speaking of it as in some sense transcendent reality, a world of being, an ὑπερουρανίος τοπός.)

(b) He might put forward a doctrine of "subsistence" of the forms, like that of Santayana in his *Realm of Essence*. I shall have to come back to this view later, and give my reasons for thinking Whitehead has been wise in rejecting it.

(c) He might define universals as recurrent types of uniformity exhibited in the process, but without any status outside it. That is to say, that given his view of the world as a multiplicity of pluralistic processes of becoming, certain types of cohesion might recur and be sustained through successive processes. This would fit in with the theory of the "laws of nature" as statistical, the average uniformities displayed through the dominant characteristics of societies of actual occasions. The whole process then may exhibit certain general uniformities and recurrent types, and, as we recognise the resemblance between these, we give them a general name.[1] This could mean that

---

[1] This, if I read him right, is the view of Professor N. Kemp Smith, in his articles "On the Nature of Universals," in *Mind*, N.S. 142, 143, 144 (vol. xxxvi.). It would be a special form of the nominalist doctrine that universals only exist *in rebus*.

the eternal object does not exist at all until it is exemplified in actuality, *i.e.* it is simply the formula, or form of definiteness, exhibited in some process; and when it has been exhibited in diverse processes, we give it a common name.

Whitehead's view was something very like this, at any rate in his earlier books. The clearest statements of it are in the chapter on "Objects" in *The Concept of Nature*, and the important chapter called "The Relatedness of Nature" in *The Principle of Relativity*. He there showed clearly that if we are to look on nature as a passage or flux of events, sense-perception and that systematisation of our perceptions which we call physical science will only be possible if there are recognisable characters sustained by the flux, since all observation implies recognition. "Recognition is that relation of the mind to nature which provides the material for the intellectual activity."[1] Even Hume, though he tries to dispose of the notion of necessary connection, has to presuppose repetition in the character of experience.[2]

The elements in nature which "do not pass," and so provide for the possibility of recognition amid passing events were called "objects." In

[1] *Concept of Nature*, p. 143.
[2] *Process and Reality*, pp. 190-191 (206-208.)

the chapter in *The Concept of Nature* different kinds of objects were distinguished — sense objects, which might be described as any recognisable data of awareness, *e.g.* blue; perceptual objects, which are relatednesses of sense objects in the events concerned, and also (apparently) considered as related to a percipient.[1] Chairs, tables, trees and stones are called perceptual objects, which are further described as " true Aristotelian adjectives " of the events in which they are situated.[2] Physical

---

[1] See " Uniformity and Contingency," *Proc. of the Aristotelian Society*, N.S., vol. xxiii., pp. 14-17.

[2] By an " Aristotelian adjective " he explains (*Uniformity and Contingency*, p. 15) he means a " pervasive " adjective, " meaning by that term an adjective of an event which is also an adjective of any temporal slice of that event. For example, a perceptual object—say a chair—which has lasted in a room for one hour, has also lasted in the room during any one minute of that hour, and so on." For an appreciative discussion of this view of Whitehead's, see F. P. Ramsey, *The Foundations of Mathematics*, pp. 127, 136-137. He argues from an analysis of the proposition " Socrates is wise " that " Socrates " and " wise " are alike adjectives of events. R. B. Braithwaite, in his review of *Science and the Modern World* (*Mind*, October, 1926), has, however, pointed out the confusion caused by Whitehead's present view of the internal relatedness of all events and eternal objects, when we try to reconcile it with this former view, of a perceptual object as an Aristotelian adjective. He then said (*Uniformity and Contingency*, p. 17) that " an Aristotelian adjective marks a breakdown of the reign of relativity ; it is just an adjective of the event which it qualifies. And this relation of adjective to subject requires no reference to anything else."

objects are described as non-delusive perceptual objects; and scientific objects are "systematic correlations of the characters of all events throughout nature." These objects were described as situated in events, or having "ingression" into them. This means that events are patient of a certain character. The events themselves are atomic and perishing, but their stream sustains certain uniformities, and repeats the pattern of their structure. In the chapter on "The Relatedness of Nature" these characters are distinguished into the general uniformities of relatedness which pervade nature, such as the systematic relations of space and time are held to be, and the contingent and "essential" characters of events. The aim of science is to exhibit so-called contingent characters of events as also dependent on systems of uniform relatedness. Thus, in the case of a factor in nature called green, it will seek to exhibit "the passage of nature in the form of a structure of events which express patience of fact for green." Yet he held there would still be "atomic" characters of events which would be independent of the character of other events. But even these, if they are to be recognisable, and so observable must be repeated throughout a route of events.[1] So what we call a "body" is the

---

[1] It must be admitted that Whitehead does not make as clear as we should like him to do the connection between this view

coherence and repetition of a pattern of objects
qualifying a given route of events. The general
character of these repetitions of the pattern displayed in events is what is called Periodicity.
There is an interesting discussion of this notion
in the *Introduction to Mathematics*, chapter xii.
Whitehead there shows that the notion of " the
essential periodicity of things," or their rhythmic
repetition, in, for instance, astronomical periods or
in vibrations and oscillations, underlies the whole
of natural science; and hence the fundamental
importance of the conception of periodic functions
in mathematics. This view is also presented by
Russell.[1] He shows that with the assimilation of
space and time to space-time, the problem of
repetition, or recognisable permanence of character
amid flux, becomes that of a periodic recurrence of
qualities. So he suggests that a physical " thing "
may be a rhythmic process, *i.e.* " a recurring cycle
of events in which there is a qualitative similarity between corresponding members of different
periods." He further says that we may distinguish
three kinds of " things "—transactions, steady
events, and rhythms. Transactions are exchanges

---

of " objects " as the permanent features of nature, and the view
in *Process and Reality* of the objective immortality of one *actual
occasion* in another. (Cf. *infra*, p. 128 *n.*)

[1] *Analysis of Matter*, chs. xxxiii. and xxxiv., especially pp. 345,
356, and 363.

6*

of energy between one process and another, according to quantum laws; steady events " continue, without internal change, from one transaction to the next, or throughout a certain portion of a continuous change; percepts are steady events, or rather systems of steady events." We may compare his view of rhythms with Whitehead's in the last chapter of the *Principles of Natural Knowledge*. "A rhythm involves a pattern and to that extent is always self-identical. But no rhythm can be a mere pattern; for the rhythmic quality depends equally upon the differences involved in each exhibition of the pattern. . . . A mere recurrence kills rhythm as surely as does a mere confusion of differences. A crystal lacks rhythm from excess of pattern, while a fog is unrhythmic in that it exhibits a patternless confusion of detail." The argument of this chapter is to show that the essence of objects called " living " is that they are rhythmic. Russell makes a fascinating suggestion of a musical analogy to the relation between " steady events " and rhythms—" that of a long note on the violin while a series of chords occurs repeatedly on the piano. All our life is lived to the accompaniment of a rhythm of breathing and heart-beating which provides us with a physiological clock by which we can roughly estimate times. I imagine, perhaps fancifully, something faintly analogous as an accompaniment to every steady event. There are laws connecting the steady event with the rhythm; these are the laws of harmony. There are laws regulating transactions; these are the laws of counterpoint."[1]

The essential point in this view of nature is to show that, while events come to pass and perish, their flux sustains permanent and recognisable characters, which make possible sense-perception and natural science, and which are described as "objects."[2] In the earlier books this difference between objects and events was simply stated as an ultimate distinction.

But in *Process and Reality* and in *Science and the Modern World* Whitehead goes much further in speculating as to the metaphysical status of these "objects," now called "eternal objects." He defines them broadly as "forms of definiteness," or "pure potentials for the specific determination of matters of fact." The metaphysical status of an eternal object is, therefore, to be a possibility for actualisation. But if it is a possibility, it is indeterminate, in the sense he gives the word in this context, as meaning not realised, or necessarily to be realised, in actuality. Yet if it is to be a "real possibility," *i.e.* effectively available for actualisation, according to the Ontological Principle it

[1] *Analysis of Matter*, p. 363.

[2] *Cf.* Russell, *op. cit.*, p. 81, on qualitative continuity as the mark of what is called a physical object.

must be grounded, that is, find a sufficient reason why it should be something, and not mere non-entity, in the nature of something actual. So he says that its mode of existence is to be "conceptually prehended" or "mentally envisaged." This is clear if we take it as meaning an envisagement by particular actualities. From the background of the data afforded me by my own past, and my relations with other events, I survey alternative possibilities, and choose the one which accords best with my purpose and valuation. This shows again the importance of the idea of final causation in the definition of an actual entity. An actual entity is a process of self-formation through its organisation of the data presented to it by the rest of the world, and its "appropriation" of these data into itself in accordance with its "subjective aim." This obviously calls for alternative possibilities; and actuality is defined as a "*decision*," in the root sense of the word, a "cutting off," or limitation among possibilities. By actualising one, it excludes other alternatives. An actual entity, as a stubborn fact, is therefore irrevocably a "decision," and limitation, whereas pure possibility as such is unbounded and undetermined. The actual entity therefore, by deciding one way, excludes alternatives which are also "forms of definiteness." So though possibilities do not exist until they are actualised, the actual entity envisages them in its decision. The course of action upon which it decides is A and might have been B.[1]

This would be clear if it simply meant that the eternal objects were possibilities envisaged by the actualities in the process of the temporal world. In so far as they are actualised, they would be types of structure displayed by actualities, and given suitable conditions, we may say that they can recur. In some cases, an actual occasion has an imaginative grasp of some possibility never before " envisaged," and so we have inventiveness, art, literature, creative advance.

[1] Of course this must not be taken as necessarily implying consciousness. It is true that Whitehead would say that consciousness emerges with the explicit recognition of alternatives— *e.g.* that A is black, and not white. But purpose, valuation and " subjective aim " are far more primary than consciousness. It is true that his doctrine that *all* actual entities are bipolar, *i.e.* have a mental as well as a physical pole, necessitates his use of what appear difficult expressions, such as " unconscious conceptual experience." But his meaning is plain. Quite apart from its crowning phase in consciousness, in every actual entity there must be the germ of originative experience which brings the possibility of alternative response to stimuli. The main point is that we should clearly understand what he means by the distinction between *conceptual* and *physical* realisation, the former being most generally described as " *appetition*," *i.e.* an originative urge for the realisation of some relevant possibility (the grasp of this possibility, or eternal object, is called " conceptual prehension." When the possibility is excluded or rejected, we have a negative prehension).

But here we come upon a part of Whitehead's view which, unless rightly understood, presents great difficulty. *There are no new eternal objects.* Creativity (the merely general, characterless, substantial activity at the base of things) brought into being as its primordial creature and characterisation a complete " envisagement " of the whole realm of eternal objects, *i.e.* the complete conceptual realisation of possibilities relevant for any process of becoming whatsoever. This is called the Primordial Nature of God; and it envisages the possibilities of all conceivable types of order, and their relevance to each actuality which can arise and be characterised through its process of becoming. But here is the difficulty. Whitehead insists on the reality of process, of creative advance, and novelty in the temporal world; and one of the necessary functions of " God " is that He should be " the organ of novelty." But this sounds as though all the novelty we can look for is the choice between alternative forms of definiteness already envisaged in the Primordial Nature of God.[1]

The difficulty becomes plain if we consider

---

[1] See, for instance, the discussion of this point in *Process and Reality*, p. 349 (377), where we are told that novelty can only come into the world through the " feeling " on the part of the temporal actual occasion of the " conceptual feelings of God."

a concrete example. A person, Whitehead would say, exhibits a certain form, or type of order, and we come upon a definition of Socrates as "a society of actual entities realising certain general systematic properties such that the Socratic predicate is realisable in that environment."[1] Does this mean that we must conclude that there is a " Socratic predicate " which is a type of order conceptually realised in the Primordial Nature of God as something which may, though not necessarily will, be physically realised? Our enjoyment—surely Whitehead's, and, one would like to speculate, God's enjoyment—of the originality of Socrates would find it hard not to be outraged if this interpretation be right. It may be said that this originality depends on the unique concurrence of (a) the Athenian Society (and this demands that "the actual world exhibits a certain systematic scheme amid which 'Athenianism' is realisable "); (b) a sub-society whose subjective aim is bold and imaginative enough to choose the " Socratic " type of order; and that these conditions can never recur again, since each type of order has to build on and conform to the order of the past. Yet if all types of order are primordially envisaged as possible for realisation there would seem to be no *a priori* reason against the recurrence of the same type, even though in fact in the case of

[1] *Op. cit.*, p. 374 (404).

an extremely complex type the probability would
be negligible.   So we might speculate as to the
possibility that—

> Another Athens shall arise
> And to remoter time
> Bequeath, like sunset to the skies,
> The splendour of its prime ;
> And leave, if nought so bright may live,
> All earth can take or Heaven can give.

It could, no doubt, be said to be a misunderstanding
to read Whitehead in this sense.   Yet his view that
the temporal process, in so far as it is characterised
and definite, is so by reason of the ingression of the
eternal objects, combined with his 3rd Category
of Explanation, that there are no new eternal
objects, and the view that all predicates are complex eternal objects,[1] might it must be admitted,
lend itself to such an interpretation.   The difficulty
arises from Whitehead's use of his Ontological
Principle.   In the 18th Category of Explanation
this is defined as meaning that actual entities are
the only reasons, so that everything in the universe
depends either on the character of some actual
entity, or on its own " subjective aim " ; and again
we are told[2] that everything is traceable to the

[1] We may remind the reader that " Socrates," on Whitehead's
view, is a predicate characterising the events constituting the
" Socratic " life.   Cf. *supra* p. 109 *n*.

[2] *Process and Reality*, p. 58 (68).

" decision " of actual entities. We are told moreover that the " decision " whereby an actual entity
forms itself (*i.e.* becomes determinate) grades the
whole multiplicity of Platonic forms in a diversity
of relevance to itself. They are potentialities,
positively or negatively prehended (*i.e.* accepted or
excluded), for realisation in that process of self-
formation. But, by an application of the Ontological Principle, we are told[1] that " the general
potentiality of the universe must be somewhere."
The notion of the " subsistence " of these potentials
is really a fudge, since it suggests that something
can float into the actual world out of nothing. It
should really stand for " the notion of how
eternal objects can be components of the primordial nature of God," and " eternal objects as in
God's primordial nature, constitute the Platonic
world of ideas." This seems to mean that when
we say that the creative advance opens up new
potentialities before itself, *i.e.* makes possible
the realisation of new types of order, it does this
through permutations and combinations of the
infinite variety of forms primordially envisaged in
" God." But it remains to be seen whether we can
disentangle the general significance of this from
the implication, which has been seen in it, that
all the æsthetic beauty, the art, friendships,

[1] *Op. cit.*, p. 63 (73).

humour, unexpectedness and remorselessnesses experienced in the process of the temporal world are simply exemplifications of " forms of definiteness " primordially envisaged.

Whitehead's view has immediately suggested, probably to a good many, that he is restating and developing the age-old answer as to the status of the Platonic Ideas, which held that they were ideas in the Mind of God.   This was the modification of Platonism first made, so far as we know, by Philo, taken from him by the Alexandrian Fathers, and given classic expression by St. Augustine. It was further developed by St. Thomas Aquinas, who has a passage on this subject worth quoting here, since it might almost be applied word for word to Whitehead's view.

" God is the *prima causa exemplaris* of all things. . . . For the production of any thing there is needed a prototype, in order that the effect may follow a determined form.   The determination of forms must be sought in the divine wisdom.   Hence one ought to say that in the divine wisdom are the *rationes* of all things; these we have called ideas, to wit prototypal forms existing in the divine mind. Although such may be multiplied in respect to things, yet really they are not other than the divine essence according as its similitude can be participated in by divers things in divers ways.   Thus God Himself is the

first exemplar of all."[1]   There is of course considerable difference in the outcome of the two views.
Whitehead would not agree with St. Thomas
that creation proceeds by the will of the primordial
cause, God, but would only claim that God provides
the subjective aims for the self-creation of actual
entities, and also the initial limitation upon mere
creativity in virtue of which there can be any
order, or process of creative advance whatsoever.
In *Religion in the Making* and the chapter on "God"
in *Science and the Modern World,* he made clear that
unfettered creativity and unbounded possibility
between them would be impotent to produce anything.   There must therefore be a primordial
limitation upon creativity, for which no sufficient
reason beyond itself can be given, but which will,
by providing an ordering of all eternal objects,
set the stage for *some* (though not necessarily
any particular) course of events.   This will be
taken up again in our last chapter.   It is God in
His function as the Principle of Concretion.

The view of the prototypal ideas as existing
in the Divine Mind was no doubt the natural
development for Platonism to have undergone,
when it was sought to bring it into logical relationship with a system of theology.   Its advantages were obvious, since (*a*) it gave an apparently

---

[1] *Summa Theologica* I, Quæs. xliv., art. 3.

reasonable answer to the difficult question as to the status of the Ideas; (*b*) it gave God a necessary place and function in the metaphysical system, which could then be used as a prolegomenon to theology, and for the vindication of religious aspiration; and (*c*) it gave the Ideas a dynamic character, since they could be looked on, not as remote abstractions, but charged with the divine love of the Thinker, and so as effective instruments in creation.

The literature and controversy which has gathered round the discussions of the relation between Plato's God and the Ideas is enough to make anyone hesitate to advance a view on this point. But at any rate it is possible to say that Plato himself did not identify the Ideas with God, nor were they in His mind. The Demiourgos of the *Timæus* looks to the αὐτὸ ὅ ἐστι ζῷον as his model, but it is not an idea in his mind. Note however that the Demiourgos, the Ideas, and the world do here need each other—the Demiourgos can only create the world by envisaging the Ideas as relevant possibilities, and it is this envisagement which makes the Ideas effective for ingression into the temporal process. We might therefore here claim a certain analogy to Whitehead's view. But on the whole we may say that Plato's theory of God is unsystematic and unmetaphysical. It is almost impossible to determine His place and function in his philosophy. (The place given Him in Whitehead's system, as the timeless source of order, seems to be taken by the Idea of the Good—though here again, the meaning of the Idea of the Good, and its relation to God is another time-honoured crux of Platonic scholarship.)

The reason seems to be that Plato, though a believer in critical definition such as the world has never seen, is prepared, when he comes to a question of ultimate religious aspiration to which no rational answer can yet be given, simply to suggest one in myth. Thus, when he is giving us metaphysical reasoning, we know that it is such; when myth and religious imagery, we also know it is such. I should not of course wish this to be taken as necessarily implying that I think that Plato held that myth was a " higher way of knowing " than rational argument, or that religious experience was from its very nature irrational (though there sometimes seems a great deal to be said for this view). I am merely concerned to point out that Plato, as distinguished from many of his followers, generally knew what he was about, so that when he gives us straight reasoning, we can recognise it as such, and when he comes to questions which he knows are not as yet soluble by straight thinking, he does not claim to be able to do so, but suggests the kind of answer which there may be in a myth, being fully aware that it is myth.

The use of the term "God" in Whitehead's philosophy makes it difficult for some readers to see what exactly he implies without bringing in a host of presuppositions and associations which would be quite foreign to his own meaning. On the other hand, metaphysics has, or should have, advanced since Plato, and, unless we take the view of religious truth as something incapable of rationalisation, we have to say that Whitehead is right in trying to formulate as clearly as possible the concept of God as it enters into his metaphysical system. He is also surely right in maintaining that rational explanation must be pushed to its furthest limits, and that there should be some point in our metaphysics which necessarily demands a natural theology, if there is to be a philosophical vindication of religion; but at the same time, it is hard to over-estimate the difficulties involved in demanding that the pre-eminently intuitive and imaginative symbolism of religion be handed over for metaphysical systematisation.

We must now return to the problem of how it is that Whitehead claims that envisagement in the Primordial Nature of God provides a status for the eternal objects apart from the temporal course of events.

We may first note that, like Plato, he seems

to be starting from an interest in the problem presented by the order in the world. Is it self-explanatory, as the relativist philosophers of Plato's day and ours would maintain, certain uniformities which are statistical averages derived from the net result of the actions and reactions and interrelations of the total multiplicity of particulars? Or can it only be rendered intelligible with reference to a timeless source of order, which transcends the particularities and contingencies of the world of becoming? I do not think that the answer is as simple as Professor Shorey would suggest, in his paper called " The Socratic Element in Plato" (read before the Sixth International Congress of Philosophy). He says that everyone is (are we to gather temperamentally?) either a materialist or he is not; and Plato, being emphatically one who was not, had to hide his transcendental spiritual reality away somewhere, so he located it in the general, abstract concept; and, in comparison with the reasonableness of this device, Professor Shorey describes Whitehead's " eternal objects in the realm of possibility " as " nephelo-coccygean." In the first place, we are tempted to ask Professor Shorey whether, as a metaphysical solution, Whitehead's view and that of Plato do not stand or fall together. In the second place, surely both Plato and Whitehead would claim more justification for the introduction of the forms than a merely arbitrary device to find a convenient hiding-place for their *Ding an sich*. But can their claim for a metaphysical justification in making the forms in some sense χωριστά —separate—be vindicated ?

Whitehead's definition of the status of the forms as possibilities to be realised in actuality has the advantage of avoiding the criticisms of the τρίτος ἄνθρωπος type—namely, as to how, if the forms and things are in different realms of being, they are to be brought into relation without some intermediary connecting link; for, if they, as well as particular things, are substances we shall want a third something which will express the resemblance between the form and the thing, and so on in an infinite regress. According to his view, the relation of the form and the process is that the former is a possibility relevant for realisation.

The most complete statement as regards the question of the relation of the forms to each other, and the structure of the realm of eternal objects, is given in the chapter on "Abstraction" in *Science and the Modern World*. It is clear that we have here a development of the Platonic notion of the κοινωνία, or interrelation of forms with each other.[1]  We start from

[1] Cf. *Sophist*, 253 *a-e*.

" the general fact of the systematic mutual relatedness inherent in the character of possibility," *i.e.* presumably, how every eternal
object is related to every other in the Primordial
Nature of God. This simply seems to mean
that, given the realisation of some possibility by
an actual occasion, all other possibilities before
that actual occasion will be graded in varying
degrees of relevance to it as compossible. But
unless we are to hold that these further possibilities are determined by the existing physical
structure of the universe, in which case there
can be no " advance into novelty," we must
say that there are possibilities which are undetermined and yet at the same time real—*i.e.*
entertained by the universe as relevant for realisation—because they are grounded in a principle
of order which transcends the already actualised
order of the temporal world.[1]   In *Process and*

[1] This may suggest the answer Whitehead would give to the
objection raised in the review of *Process and Reality* in *Mind*,
October, 1930 (by Miss Stebbing), and in an article by Mr. Hill
of the University of Chicago in a recent number of the *Journal
of Philosophy*, entitled " Of What Use are Whitehead's Eternal
Objects ?"   It is claimed that all the functions Whitehead
formerly ascribed to " objects " (identity, repetition, permanence,
abstraction) are in his present system fully accounted for by
actual entities, owing to the doctrine of the objectification of
one actual entity in another.   Whitehead here indeed insists
that apart from some ordering of possibilities transcending
those actually realised in the temporal world, there can be no

*Reality*[1] this order is described as "transcendent decision," *i.e.* God's Primordial Nature is a "conceptual realisation," in the sense Whitehead always gives this phrase, namely a conceptual envisagement of eternal objects together with an "appetition" towards their physical realisation. God therefore brings the eternal objects into relation to the temporal world in two ways. (*a*) He is the ground transcending the temporal world, for pos-

---

explanation of novelty and creative advance. It is therefore necessary for him still to maintain a distinction between actual entities and eternal objects. But the doctrine of the objective immortality of actual entities, in their character as superjects of their own subjective experience, in the constitution of other actual entities is, as Miss Stebbing points out, a departure from the earlier view of events as particular and transient, and objects alone as able to "be again." This difficulty would however be mitigated if we could say (as Whitehead himself however nowhere does, as far as I know) that it is not actual entities which are objectively immortal in the constitution of other actual entities, but the *characters*, or *forms* of their experience which are reproduced (*cf. infra*, Ch. VII., p. 187). The notion of "present immediacy" is more consistent with this, and it also would accord with the earlier view of "objects." The only way of interpreting these views in answer to Miss Stebbing's very legitimate difficulty in the passage in *Process and Reality*, [p. 66 (76)], in which the Ontological Principle is said to "blur the sharp distinction between what is universal and what is particular," would be to say that since the eternal objects are realised in the conceptual experience of a particular actual entity (God), they are no longer subsistent universals.

[1] P. 229 (248).

sibilities as yet unrealised in it. (*b*) He brings what would otherwise be simply abstract, " subsistent " forms into *effective* relevance to the temporal world, by providing at the same time the appetition towards their realisation. Since this transcendent principle of order contains more than a mere " multiplicity " of disconnected forms, each possibility realised will open up all others either as relevant for realisation, or as excluded as incompatible.[1] Exclusion of eternal objects by actual entities is called negative prehension. Since the reason for an exclusion is to be found in the nature of the actual entity and the eternal object taken together, Whitehead holds that a negative prehension (*i.e.* definite exclusion on the ground of mutual incompatibility) constitutes a " bond," or form of relatedness.

In view of this general fact of the relatedness of all eternal objects, Whitehead has to deal with the problem of the sense in which we may say that some are more " relevantly " related than others. Otherwise we are involved in the difficulty of monistic logicians, of not being able to say anything about anything without saying everything about everything, or, in other words, in the problem of finite truth. Whitehead's solution of this is to say that the general scheme

[1] *Cf.* the view in the *Sophist* that some classes do not communicate with each other.

of relatedness of the realm of eternal objects does not require the "individual essence," as he calls it, or "what the eternal object is in itself," as distinguished from its relational essence," which is the eternal object considered as related to others, and as potential for ingression into actual occasions.[1] So we have a general systematic background implied in all eternal objects, and within this sub-realms or hierarchies of inter-related eternal objects, each of which can be considered in abstraction from parallel hierarchies, though not from the general relatedness which is the common systematic background of them all.

The relation of the whole realm to actuality

[1] *Science and the Modern World*, ch. x., pp. 221 *sq.* It may be remarked that whenever Whitehead speaks of internal relations, his exact meaning is very obscure. He is unwilling to accept the consequences of an out-and-out monism, and yet insists that " the relatednesses of an event are all internal relations" (*Science and the Modern World*, p. 174). The difficulties have been brought out in the review of *Science and the Modern World* in *Mind*, October, 1926. It appears that while every event positively prehends every other, it only positively prehends a selection of eternal objects so that finite true propositions can be made about it. But it is to be regretted that he does not show the relation between the view here, and that of the " essential," " contingent " and " atomic " characters of events described in the chapter on " The Relatedness of Nature " (cf. *supra*, p. 110). See also " Uniformity and Contingency " (Presidential Address to the Aristotelian Society, 1922), *Proceedings of the Aristotelian Society*, N.S., vol. xxiii., p. 17.

is as a scheme of possibilities of varying degrees of relevance. So an actuality $x$ prehending A will prehend, through RR′, "the whole sweep of eternal relatedness," though it will obviously prehend B and C as of more immediate relevance than D, E, F, and the relevance of G, H, I may be so remote as to be negligible. ABC might be called a complex eternal object. If we went on building a more and more complex structure on the base of the simple eternal object

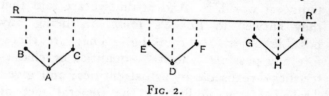

FIG. 2.

A, it could be called an abstractive hierarchy. Each actual occasion prehending A will have its "associated hierarchy" of eternal objects. But the general form of relatedness RR′ is incumbent upon all participants in the eternal objects. It would seem to consist in the metaphysical principles of absolute generality.

But when we come to the sub-hierarchies of forms within RR′, it is clear that Whitehead intends them to include far more than this. It might be tempting to restrict the realm of eternal objects to the general logico-mathematical forms implied in the structure of things; and in this case we could say that Whitehead was working out what, according at any rate to some of his commentators, was Plato's own final view. But it is clear from *Process and Reality* that Whitehead means far more than this by the eternal objects. They are defined[1] as " Pure Potentials for the Specific Determination of Fact "—" Forms of definiteness "—and again[2] as " Any entity whose conceptual recognition does not involve a necessary reference to any definite actual entities of the temporal world."[3] And again, we are told that they answer to Locke's ideas, in being any possible objects of thinking. They are therefore any possible " hows "—qualities or characteristics—realisable by actual entities; and given " relevant " possibility by the general fact of systematic relatedness underlying both the eternal objects already realised in the temporal world, and those which are still undetermined potentials awaiting realisation.

If, however, we could have taken the interpretation of the eternal objects as simply the logico-mathematical forms of most complete generality, we might have had an answer to the problem raised above, namely how far they are literally to be taken as archetypes or patterns of all possible courses of events. But as it is, we must probably

---

[1] *Op. cit.*, p. 29 (32).  [2] *Ibid.*, p. 60 (70).
[3] *Ibid.*, p. 72 (82).

simply say that this is a point that Whitehead has not made clear. His continual insistence on novelty and originality in the becoming of actual entities shows that he would not wish to be understood as implying a simple "copying" theory. On the other hand, the passages here considered show that he means that *some* eternal object or form of definiteness must enter into every actuality in *every* respect in which it achieves definiteness or determination. Eternal objects are said to include even the determinate ways in which the actual entity organises its prehension of eternal objects in its own process of self-formation, so changing the generality of forms " conceptually prehended " into the original particularity of physical existence.

Thus on pp. 412-414 (445-447) of *Process and Reality* the eternal objects are divided into subjective and objective. The latter alone could bear any possible analogy to the Platonic Ideas. They are qualities or characteristics realisable in actual entities.

The former are *characters* of subjective forms —*i.e. how* actual entities prehend other actual entities or eternal objects, the different qualitative ways in which feelings are felt. Since these also are potentials, they are classed as eternal objects. And correspondingly we are told[1] that

[1] *Op. cit.*, p. 330 (356).

the realm of eternal objects includes abstract intensive patterns (*i.e.* of the "hows" of feelings) as well as abstract qualitative patterns. Plato represents Socrates in the *Parmenides* as shocked at the thought of admitting Ideas of mud and hair into his heaven of forms. He might have been still more shocked at Whitehead's unrestricted immigration policy. Whitehead is however simply applying consistently his notion of eternal objects as *all possible* "hows" of definiteness.

Now that I have been attempting to bring out the analogies and distinctions which might be drawn between the Platonic Ideas, and Whitehead's eternal objects, it should be made clear that in so doing I have been unable to consider one whole side of Whitehead's thought, namely that in which he analyses the concept of Process. The result of taking this into account is that while general analogies may be drawn, the total emphasis and final point of view in Whitehead's metaphysics is very different, at any rate from what has generally come to be understood as Platonism. To Whitehead "Process" and "Reality" imply and demand one another. The eternal objects are simple potentials for realisation in the becoming of actualities. An actuality is described as a process of becoming, or experiencing, in which it arises as an organic synthesis, a self-formation, out of its relations to the rest of the universe including the order of eternal objects. There is thus no dualism between the realms of Being and Becoming.

Plato is, however, not so very far from such a conception in his discussion of Being and Not-Being in the *Sophist*. In criticising the " friends of the forms," who deny the power of acting and being acted upon to Being, he shows that such a complete separation of Being from process, or movement (perhaps, though this is a word to be used advisedly, we might say from experience), leads to an *impasse* between the Idealists and Materialists. He then suggests a definition of Being as anything with the capacity of acting or being acted upon (δύναμις).[1] We may compare Whitehead's 4th Category of Explanation,[2] where it is said that it belongs to the nature of " being " that it is a potential for every " becoming." He calls this the most general statement of " the principle of relativity "—namely that the nature of an actuality is defined by the way in which it can enter as a constituent into other actualities.[3]

The dialogue in the *Sophist* then goes on[4] to say

[1] 247*e*.

[2] *Process and Reality*, p. 30 (33).

[3] Cf. *ibid.*, p. 39 (43). We may recall again Locke's statement of this principle in his *Essay* Book II., xxiii., 7, where he says *powers* form a great part of our complex ideas of substance.

[4] 249*a*.

7

that in this case we must agree that motion, life and mind belong to Being. "And, O heavens, can we ever be made to believe that motion and life and soul and mind are not present with absolute Being? Can we imagine Being to be devoid of life and mind, and to remain in awful unmeaningness, an everlasting fixture?" (Jowett's translation). Here we have a vehement expression of an idea which reappears in Whitehead's repudiation of "vacuous actuality,"[1] *i.e.* of Being which has no subjective experience.

We here seem also to be approaching the idea of the Primordial Nature of God; *i.e.* Plato seems here to be criticising heavily the view of the forms as static, detached essences. If they are Being, they must be set in motion by life and mind; or, as Whitehead would say, it is only through a "conceptual evaluation" that the forms can become effective possibilities for realisation in temporal events; and without it there would be no sufficient reason for any course of events whatsoever.

The discussion which then follows in the *Sophist* concerning which different "categories" (γενή) can communicate with one another and which cannot, results in the conclusion that Rest and Motion, Same and Other all communicate in Being, and that of these five "kinds," Being and

---

[1] *Process and Reality,* pp. 39 (43), 234 (253), 438 (471).

Other are all-pervasive. The search for the universal " kinds " in which all things participate is
held to be the peculiar work of the philosopher.[1]
Here we may compare Whitehead's view of metaphysics as an attempt to formulate the ultimate
generalities.[2]

He would also fully agree with Plato's saying[3]
that the sceptics who take the purely atomic point
of view, that nothing " participates " in anything
else, are, like the ventriloquist Eurycles, refuted
out of their own bellies, since everything we do
and say presupposes interdependence and derivation.[4]   Hence the rigid separation of one thing
from another, a refusal to inquire into the ways in
which things "partake of" and "communicate in "
each other, with its outcome in a delight in paradoxes for their own sake, is the mark of the Sophist
and not of the Philosopher.[5]   Those of us who
find Whitehead's metaphysics difficult may perhaps be consoled by the further distinction,[6] that
the Sophist hides in the darkness of Not-Being, in
which he is accustomed to find his way about, but

[1] 253*d*.

[2] *Process and Reality*, p. 11 (12).

[3] 252*c*.

[4] Cf. *Process and Reality*, p. 247 (267) ; and the discussions
of causal and " vector " feelings, *passim*.

[5] 259*d* ; *cf*. Whitehead, *Process and Reality*, Pt. I., ch. i.,
" Speculative Philosophy," especially §§ 1 and 2.

[6] 254*a*.

" the philosopher always holding converse through reason with the idea of Being is also dark from excess of light."

*Note.*—I have not been able to enter into a discussion of a kind of view which has also been claimed as Platonic, and as akin to Whitehead's: namely the doctrine of subsistence of the Critical Realists, and in particular Santayana's Realm of Essence. I will merely point out in passing that this kind of view seems to me a degenerate form of Platonism, for the following reasons:

(*a*) The " essences " completely fail to fulfil what was to Plato a necessary function of the forms, namely to give an explanation of what broken bits of order we find in the world of becoming, so that by starting from these it might be possible to rise to knowledge of the timeless causes of order. But Santayana's essences have no necessary connection, no " participation " in the world of becoming. As regards this world, we are therefore left in complete scepticism, or have to circumvent its shocks by " animal faith."

(*b*) The doctrine of essences as " subsisting " seems to be little more than a verbal trick to obtain the advantages of the transcendent status of universals without facing its difficulties, a kind of metaphysical representation without taxation.

(*c*) Santayana contrasts his " democracy " of essences with Plato's (and presumably Whitehead's) "aristocracy"—*i.e.* graded hierarchy of forms. To Plato and Whitehead, the realm of forms, as the source of order which was for "the best," would necessarily contain sub-hierarchies subordinate to those which were sources of subtler and richer types of order.

Santayana may claim[1] to have shaken himself free from Plato's ethical prejudice, but whether it be prejudice or not, it seems clear to me, if my reading of him is right, that an "aristocracy" among the Ideas is an integral part of Plato's thought, and cannot be removed from it without changing his whole meaning. On the other hand, Santayana's Realm of Essences, completely democratic and individualistic, and in no necessary connection with anything that exists, seems to me little other than (to use, I think, a phrase of Whitehead's) "a metaphysical mare's nest."

[1] See, *e.g.*, his *Platonism and the Spiritual Life.*

# CHAPTER VI

## THE ORGANISATION OF FEELINGS

### Gefuhl ist alles.—FAUST.

IT will be recalled that Whitehead says that he holds the central discovery of the Kantian philosophy to be that an act of experience is a construction.[1]  But where his Philosophy of Organism parted company from Kant was in saying that what is constructed is not an objective world out of the experience of the subject, but primarily the subject itself, which is constructed according to the way in which it feels its objective world.  So he says " in Cartesian language " " the essence of an actual entity consists solely in the fact that it is a prehending thing."[2]  That is to say, if we are to take the concept of process seriously, a " thing " is simply the becoming or growth of a new way of feeling the rest of the world.  It will be noted that we here use the term " feeling " as synonymous with " prehension."[3]  It is used in this way throughout the latter part of *Process and Reality*, as covering every kind of relation which he described as " positive prehension,"

[1] Cf. *supra*, p. 48.       [2] *Process and Reality*, p. 56 (65).
[3] Cf. *ibid.*, p. 312 (337) and p. 55 (65),

*i.e.* any action of one entity upon another. So, substituting the word " feeling " in the above definition, we can say that " the essence of an actual entity consists in the fact that it is a feeling thing." A concrete actual entity is an act of experience; and Whitehead, like Bradley, claims that this must imply some kind of sentience.[1] He goes so far as to say[2] that an actual fact is at bottom a fact of æsthetic experience. We can here refer to what he calls " The Category of Subjective Intensity," which states that since actual entities are " drops of experience " some degree of intensity of feeling is the common denominator of all actuality. (We shall later on have reason to suggest that Whitehead's metaphysic is founded primarily not on considerations drawn from physics, or mathematical logic, but on æsthetics.)

The Philosophy of Organism aspires therefore to construct "*a critique of pure feeling*."[3] " Feeling " may in some ways be an unfortunate term, as suggesting higher grades of experience, or even the so-called " intellectual feelings " which are conscious. But he is using it as a general term to express the fundamental and primitive

[1] Cf. *supra*, p. 80.
[2] *Religion in the Making*, p. 115; cf. *Process and Reality*, p. 395 (426).
[3] *Process and Reality*, p. 158 (172).

thing about experience, which is that it is "emotional—blind emotion—received as felt elsewhere in another occasion."[1] This is the kind of feeling which in its higher stages we may call sympathy; but it might be misleading to use this as a general term. It follows from the view of an actual occasion as an atomic "drop of experience," arising from its prehensions of the rest of its world, that if he is to say that an actual occasion reproduces features of other occasions in itself (" objectification "), this must be described as the feeling of the feelings of other actual occasions. We must bear in mind that "feeling" is here used throughout as the purely general term for any kind of acting or being acted upon, in such a way that the make-up of the subject is affected. In Whitehead's own words, it is "the basic generic operation of passing from the objectivity of the data to the subjectivity of the actual entity in question."[2]

So "causation" becomes the reproduction in one actual occasion of the feelings of another, or, more precisely, the conformity of the feelings of the present occasion to the feelings of others. This is particularly important in the case of those routes of successive occasions we call an enduring object—for instance, an animal body over a

[1] *Op. cit.*, p. 227 (246), and see also p. 55 (65).
[2] *Ibid.*, p. 55 (65).

certain interval of time. In this case, we have not simply a bare succession of atomic occasions, but a peculiarly full objectification of each successive occasion into the next, so that there is a continual reproduction and conformity of feelings.

A natural and immediate reaction to this kind of view is to say that it is a glaring example of the pathetic fallacy—an interpretation of the whole of nature in terms only applicable to highly developed stages of experience. Are we to take seriously the statement[1] that wave-lengths and vibrations are simply terms, under the abstractions of physics, for " pulses of emotion "? The only answer is that we must take our choice. We may agree with Whitehead, Bergson, Bradley, that philosophy must approach as near as possible to an expression of the concrete, and that concrete reality is meaningless except as some form of sentient experience, and in this case some view like this, which describes the organic connections between things in terms of something like feeling, is inevitable. If we can find a general term which is less suggestive of pathetic fallacies, so much the better. It is, for instance, certainly very difficult to get used to thinking of the geometrical relations of anything as the "feeling of a strain."[2] Perhaps it would have been better if he had kept to

[1] *Op. cit.*, p. 228 (247).
[2] *Ibid.*, Pt. IV., ch. iv.

the less misleading because more technical term " positive prehension."[1]

The alternative, with for instance Russell, and most of the modern realists, is to look on all this kind of philosophy as hopelessly anthropomorphic; and to hold that we are not justified in going beyond logic and the language of physical science; that this is concerned simply with what is publicly observable, and to go behind this to views about the subjective nature of actuality takes us into a region of mysticism, where it is illegitimate to claim that our guesses are serious philosophy. We must, I have said, take our choice; or rather, since the choice is very difficult, perhaps impossible, if it implies a rigorous exclusion of the other alternative, we must see how much there is to be said for either type of philosophy after its own kind, and hold that a systematic development of each by different philosophers is likely to be valuable. No doubt in the end we need an attempt at a synthetic philosophy on Whitehead's lines; but while the basic ideas of almost all branches of modern thought are in so tentative and transitional a state, there is everything to be said for a good many philosophers persisting with the more pedestrian, analytic method. But we should see the point in what each is trying to do, and not

---

[1] Cf. *loc. cit.*, pp. 311-312 (337).

dismiss the former kind of philosophy as mythological nonsense, or the latter as mere logical
hair-splitting.

We must return from this digression to the
theory of feelings as a theory of the self-formation
of actual entities.  It will be impossible to go in
any detail into the discussion of the various types
of feeling which Whitehead distinguishes.  They
are set out in *Process and Reality*, Part III.  In
the latter part of this chapter, I shall simply touch
on the theory of feeling as it affects Whitehead's
views in epistemology.  In the next chapter, I
shall be considering the theory of feeling as it
affects his view of the emergence of definite and
recognisable types of nexūs of actual entities
in the physical world.  In both these chapters
it will be necessary to refer from time to time to
the " Categoreal (*sic*) Obligations."[1]  These are
the conditions, according to Whitehead's Categorical Scheme, to which any process of becoming
must conform, *i.e.* they are necessary characteristics of any such process.  It may well be felt
that there is a certain arbitrariness about them.
Why should there be just nine, and why must
they be incumbent on any process whatsoever ?
But we can only recall what was said at the end of
Chapter II. about Whitehead's method in setting
out his scheme.  It is not a dictatorial or *a priori*

[1] *Process and Reality*, Pt. I., ch. ii., § 3.

assertion of first principles, but a formulation of general ideas which have been wrought out of a long series of critical enquiries. So the " Categoreal Obligations " are characteristics which have seemed to Whitehead essential in anything which may be called an actual process of becoming. We may not be prepared to accept them all as they stand; but at any rate they form a valuable table of reference for his basic ideas.

The first point about which we must be quite clear, in considering Whitehead's theory of feeling, is the distinction between conceptual and physical feelings. This is simply a statement, in different terms, and a rather fuller form, of the distinction between physical and conceptual prehension.[1] It must be remembered that he holds that an actual entity is always dipolar. Its " physical pole " is its feeling of other actual entities; its " mental pole " is its feeling of eternal objects, which is here called " conceptual feeling." Whitehead holds that we must say that every actuality has a mental pole, though in the vast majority it is dormant or almost negligible. Therefore we must not confuse " conceptual feelings " with the relatively small class of intellectual feelings called conscious. A conceptual feeling is any feeling of an eternal object; that is to say, any grasp of a new possibility. Whether

[1] Cf *supra*, Ch. V., p. 115 *n*.

or no he is justified in using the term " conceptual "
for an unconscious feeling, it is clear that Whitehead is maintaining that we must make this distinction between a merely passive being acted upon
by other actual entities (physical feeling), and some
form of originative response, which, as involving
new possibilities, involves what he calls a feeling
of eternal objects (conceptual feeling). This
latter kind of feeling he sometimes describes by
the general term " appetition."[1]   This is defined
as " an urge towards the future based on an
appetite in the present."   He suggests that this
is the most fundamental thing about nature.
Things grow because of a feeling of something
as yet unrealised, yet present in the form of an
urge towards realisation.   He gives thirst as an
example at a low level.[2]   It drives an organism
to seek some sort of relief, and so to promote its
life, whereas the unchecked physical tendency
would lead to its being dried up.   In a conceptual feeling the new element is felt as desired
in the immediate present or the *relevant* future.
We meet here another important notion, that of
*relevance*.   Some factors in the future are anticipated as contributors to the subject's own intensity.
Whitehead says that it is here that we tread on

[1] *Cf.* Leibniz' use of this term, for the active unfolding of
the potentialities of the Monad.

[2] *Function of Reason*, p. 72.

the border of morals—in the determination of
what is really relevant; *i.e.* consistent with the
subjective aim as directed towards richness of
order.   But this is to anticipate.

Besides pure physical and conceptual feelings,
Whitehead admits a third class called " hybrid
physical feelings."[1]   This notion is insufficiently
explained and seems very obscure.   Presumably
it means the feeling of an eternal object felt by
another actual entity; for instance, if I feel the
tree as green, I am feeling the tree as prehending
conceptually the eternal object green.   But this
was provided for by " The Category of Conceptual
Valuation," which stated that from the physical
feeling of a nexus (the tree) is derived a conceptual
feeling of the eternal object characterising it
(green).   On the other hand " The Category of
Conceptual Reversion " stated that there is a
feeling of the distinction of eternal objects,
prehended in the former manner (according to the
Category of Conceptual Valuation) from others also
grasped as " relevant to the Subjective Aim," *i.e.*
which the subject is capable of prehending, or which
fall within its universe of discourse.   So there is
a feeling of " green when you would like it to
be brown," or " green and not-brown." (This
feeling of a distinction between realised eternal
objects and unrealised alternatives is very impor-

---

[1] *Process and Reality*, Pt. III., ch. ii.

tant.    Whitehead holds that it is the beginning of consciousness.)    A hybrid feeling might be a feeling of the tree as entertaining the possibility of being brown—then " brown " would be an eternal object conceptually felt by the tree.    The only clear statement of what a hybrid physical feeling may be is *Process and Reality* p. 349 (377), where we are told that in feeling eternal objects we have hybrid physical feelings of God, since all eternal objects are conceptually prehended by God, of whom we have physical feelings because He is an actual entity.    This is certainly an illustration of how far from our usual forms of expression Whitehead's terminology can take us. Whether theories like this have really any important significance it is too early to judge.    We must wait until they have been ventilated for longer, and we have become more used to this very unusual kind of language.    At any rate to say, out of the context of *Process and Reality*, that when I say " red " I am indulging in a hybrid physical feeling of God, sounds startling enough.    This is not necessarily to condemn it, for a theory has to be judged in its context.    But it is enough to indicate the difficulty in importing Whitehead's views quickly into our philosophical or theological discussions.

But we must leave this, and turn to the consideration of Whitehead's discussions of perception in the light of his theory of feelings.  His view of perception is most fully described in *Symbolism*;[1] and specifically discussed in *Process and Reality*, Part II., chs. ii. and viii. (on " The Extensive Continuum " and " Symbolic Reference "). Certain features in it may be noted which are interesting, and on the whole new, contributions to the problem.

In the first place, it divides perception into two modes, " causal efficacy," and " presentational immediacy."  Whitehead makes the former prior and more fundamental.  This is very important, as his view both of the evidence for the existence of an external world, and of the notion of " cause " depends upon it.  For if we take the concept of process seriously, all that we actually have at any time are the passing events of present immediacy.  But in these we cannot get away from the feeling of an immediate derivation and influence, say from the events of a quarter of a second ago.  This feeling of derivation means that an actual entity cannot be complete in itself, but must have what he calls a " vector " reference beyond itself.  So nothing " needs only itself in order to exist," and causation is an assertion of this principle.  It is not an assertion of un-

---

[1] *Symbolism : Its Meaning and Effect* (Cambridge, 1928). Barbour-Page Lectures given at the University of Virginia in 1927.

changing causal laws, or of forces pushing and
pulling, but simply of the fact that actual entities
are so related that what happens in one is dependent on what happens in another.    Certain
(though not necessarily all) changes in the characters of diverse groups of actual entities are thus
correlated.    The Philosophy of Organism claims
that this is fundamental to what we know of
nature: the insistence that " causal efficacy " is
primary in perception is an example.

There is a feeling, perhaps blind and vague,
of relevance to a world of the immediate past,
and to the immediate background from which
the actual occasion is emerging.    The theory
of perception depends on the clear distinction
between this feeling of causal efficacy, and the
*contemporary* world of the actual entity.    Here
contemporary is defined, in what is apparently
the sense suggested by the Theory of Relativity,
as " causal independence."    When two events
arise in such a way that they *cannot* affect one
another, they are contemporaneous (*e.g.* light
may not have had time to be transmitted from
one to the other).    This definition clearly does
not imply that two events which are contemporaneous with the same event are necessarily contemporaneous with each other.[1]    So in perception

---

[1] For the ultimate character of the notion of Simultaneity,
*cf.* Whitehead's paper in the *Proceedings of the Aristotelian*

we are claiming to see something in the contemporary world. What we are really doing is
using symbolically a feeling of something in the
immediate past and referring it to something
in the present. This " something " in the immediate past is a sense-datum, for instance a colour,
which we take to symbolise a contemporary chair.
It comes from the immediate past, because,
Whitehead holds, it depends on the state of the
body. The nexus of occasions called the body
is affected in a certain way by other occasions
external to them, which then objectify their
feelings in the " percipient occasion," which is
the " presiding personality at that moment in the
body."[1] This then interprets these feelings of
colour, smell, sound etc., as having symbolic
reference to a world of presentational immediacy.
Note that this depends on the view that the body
is really affected by other things (*i.e.* on the priority
of causal efficacy)—feelings, as he puts it, have

---

*Society* (Suppl. vol. iii.), entitled " On the Problem of Simultaneity." See also the paper " Time, Space and Material "
(Suppl. vol. ii.), in which there is a clear statement of the distinction between the creative advance of nature and the multiplicity of the different time-systems belonging to different nexūs
of events, with its corollary that two event-particles which are
simultaneous for time-system α will not in general be simultaneous for another time-system α'.

[1] This notion of a "presiding personality" will be discussed
in the next chapter.

a "vector" reference to a datum felt—and on the view that these feelings are transmitted *via* the body to the percipient occasion. In most ordinary perception the transmission is so nearly instantaneous that reference to presentational immediacy is very seldom mistaken. But it does involve the possibility of error, as when we see a patch of colour and refer it to an event in the contemporary sky, whereas it really results from the causal efficacy of light reaching the eye from a star which went out of existence a thousand years before. Both error and progress in communication are made possible by symbolic reference.

An interesting feature of this view is Whitehead's theory about the so-called "sense-data"—colours and sounds, and so forth. In his earlier work he had protested firmly against a "bifurcation of nature," *i.e.* any view which divides nature into primary and secondary qualities, the latter being in some way dependent on mind, or on awareness. This was naturally taken to mean that all relatedness, on which "qualities" etc. are held to depend, is a relatedness of a situation in nature. Secondary qualities are not relative to a different kind of entity called "mind." This sort of view might be described as "objective relativism."[1] But the "sense-

[1] *Cf.* A. E. Murphy, "Objective Relativism in Dewey and Whitehead" (*Philosophical Review*, 1927).

data " are now described as feelings of some
form of definiteness derived by the perceiving
subject through the immediate past of its body.
(Hence illusory perceptions are traced to physiological conditions.)   The body is just the most
immediately relevant part of the environment
of a percipient occasion.[1]   These sense-data,
as feelings of some form of definiteness, are then
treated as eternal objects predicated of some part
of the contemporary world.   Thus he says[2] that
colours may be considered either as sensations
or as qualities.   A colour when we see it is part
of the make-up of the percipient (and in this sense
a sensation), but we refer it as a quality to the
wall out there.[3]   Here are some obvious difficulties, most of which are discussed in the chapter
entitled " Mr. Whitehead and the Denial of
Simple Location " in R. O. Lovejoy's book *The
Revolt against Dualism*.   I shall refer in the next
chapter to his criticisms of what is meant by
" simple location " (with most of which I find
myself in complete agreement).   I will simply
point out here, with regard to his discussion of
the more immediate question of perception, that
he may be right in maintaining that this development of Whitehead's view departs from the denial
of the " bifurcation of nature," as interpreted in

[1] *Process and Reality*, Pt. II., ch. ii., and *Symbolism*, pp. 58 *sq.*
[2] *Symbolism*, p. 25.                    [3] *Ibid.*, p. 18.

the extreme realist sense of putting all percepta
" out there " in nature; but not as holding that
all percepta and the percipient are together in
one relational complex within nature.[1]

The view of perception is now more complicated.
We have (a) the influence of certain actual entities
of the environment on the actual entities of the
more immediate environment of a percipient occasion, which are called its animal body, and this
objectification into the animal body described
in terms of feelings called " sense-data "; (b) the
objectification from the entities of the body of
these sense-data into the immediately supervening
" percipient occasion " (which, whether seriously
or not, Whitehead suggests may be wandering
about in the interstices of the brain, enjoying a
peculiar richness of inheritance from the whole
of the body); (c) the using of these sense-data by
the percipient occasion as symbols for something
in presentational immediacy.    Lovejoy suggests
that with the introduction of the mediating sense-
data, Whitehead has gone back on his denial of
the bifurcation of nature, in favour of some form
of dualism.[2]    But we may observe that there is
no difference in *kind* between the sense-data and
the objects to which they are referred.    They are
simply feelings transmitted through the body,

[1] Cf. *Science and the Modern World*, pp. 77, 127.
[2] *Op. cit.*, p. 188.

and used as symbols for the external events, whose immediate predecessors were felt by the body. We thus have a unity of experience, within which some elements are used as symbols of others. Symbolism does not imply dualism.

A more serious objection (though the former, if it were valid, Lovejoy would consider a commendation rather than an objection) is that Whitehead is simply giving us in very complicated language a comparatively common-sense view. But it must be remembered that he has to state his view in terms of the theory of feelings, and also to safeguard himself from speaking of either the percipient occasion or the object of perception as enduring substances. Since each is, by definition, a process, and, as contemporaneous, causally independent of the other, one can only perceive the other through the reproduction of its characteristics through the successive occasions of the environment. These would be firstly waves of light, then the occasions organised in the neural structure of the animal body—until finally they affect the percipient occasion. They are then inferred to be characteristics of entities of the contemporary environment, which have immediately supervened upon, and so in all probability reproduced, the characteristics of the originally transmitting entities. This at least is the only way in which I can see how sense-data can be described both as eternal objects (*i.e.* qualities) and as sensations.

The important contribution of the view seems to me to be the clear insistence, which is surely right, on causal efficacy as the prior factor—the feeling of other things as affecting one. And if, with Hume, we call these simply " impressions arising from unknown causes," Whitehead points out that sensations of the bodily organs, " hearing with the ears " and so on, are as inexplicable as consciousness of a more remote environment. Merely private sensation could be conscious of *nothing*. If this be so, the problem of perception should be, not to discuss whether private sensations refer to an external world, but to exhibit how the feelings produced in us by external things of the immediate past can be used symbolically as means of inferring something about the present, and of making possible communication with others about the nature of a common external world.

Moreover there is an important statement[1] as to the nature of symbolic reference, which makes it clear that symbols to be valuable must have some " intersection " with the symbolised—*i.e.* some element of their structure in common. That is to say, the process of abstraction of certain features, which attract our attention in the concrete passage of nature, is not a purely arbitrary one. The

[1] *Symbolism*, p. 58.

passage has some persistent properties which permit of its being analysed in this way. In the case of the " sense-data " this must mean that the percipient's feeling of them through the bodily organs must conform, to some extent at any rate, with the original feeling by those organs, which should in turn have been determined by the nature of the object felt. So a sense-datum, as an " eternal object " must reduce itself to the *form* (or character) of a feeling transmitted by various occasions to each other. If the symbolism is to give any valid information, the form of feeling as received by the percipient occasion must still conform in some respect to the form as originally qualifying the object, and as transmitted by the object to its own succeeding events.

In considering the nature of the abstractive process involved in perception, we should refer to the 4th " Categoreal Obligation," called " The Category of Transmutation." This states that any objects which we can perceive will not be actual entities, but large societies or nexūs of actual entities. In this case, what happens is that there is a feeling of many actual entities with a similar conceptual valuation. Thus an average character of the nexus as a whole is elicited, and we generalise as to the eternal object characterising it—*e.g.* " the tree is green." (Whitehead points out that atomic philosophies always have a difficulty in

showing how groups can have a common characteristic.)   We must think of the transmission of
feelings as involving a very complicated process
of abstraction of this kind, so that in the end
all that is felt is an attenuated general character
of the original nexus, which is then applied as a
generalised predicate to the nexus as a whole.   But
even after this attempt, it is nevertheless a shock
to think that when we perceive, for instance, a
stone, we have in the end to say that we are " feeling the feelings " in the stone.

But this is necessitated by Whitehead's view of
the transmission of feelings.   " Objectification," or
the entry of actual entities into the constitution of
one another, was described in terms of conformity
and reproduction of their feelings.   This we saw
might naturally be described as " sympathy,"
if this were not an even more anthropomorphic
and misleading term than " feeling " (used in
Whitehead's generalised sense).   But this gives
rise to the very legitimate difficulty pointed out in
the review of *Process and Reality* in *Mind*—namely,
his failure to explain the connection between the
present view of the objective immortality of actual
entities through their objectification in others, and
his earlier view (*e.g.* in *The Concept of Nature*) that
it is only objects, and not events, which can " be
again."[1]   According to the theory of transmission

[1] Cf. *supra*, p. 128 *n.*

of feelings, "objectification" means the reproduction in one actual entity of the feeling in another. But the word "feeling" can surely only legitimately be used of something transient, and existing only in the present immediacy of an actual entity. That same feeling cannot "be again" through objective immortality in other actual entities. According to this interpretation, therefore, the doctrine of the objectification of feelings would be a loose way of saying that the feeling in one actual entity reproduces the *character*, or quality, of the feeling in the other actual entities which it feels. This "character" or "quality" would be what he formerly described as an "object," so that there would not then need to be any real departure from his earlier view. But the whole emphasis of these discussions in *Process and Reality* goes to show that Whitehead does now mean that the actual *feeling* of one actual entity is objectified and reproduced in another. The Subjective Form is the feeling of the subject, derived from its objects and re-directed upon them. It is however to be regretted that Whitehead does not explicitly state the departure from and connection with his previous view.

We pass now to the class of feelings called "Propositional." Whitehead has rather an interesting and original view of propositions, which is developed at some length in *Process and Reality*,

Part II., chapter ix. Propositions were also included among the Categories of Existence, as being a new kind of entity, midway between eternal objects, which are pure potentials, and particular actual entities. They were called " Matters of Fact in Potential Determination," or " Impure Potentials for the Specific Determination of Matters of Fact." It is again a little hard to see why they should be a special Category of Existence— they are rather one of the modes of existence produced by the coming together of actual entities and eternal objects. The notion of an eternal object is that of a possibility. It is a possible form of definiteness for actuality, e.g. I prehend blueness as realised here and possible elsewhere. So eternal objects are related to the actual world as potentials for it. Now in a propositional feeling there is the integration of the physical feeling of an actual entity with a conceptual feeling of an eternal object or complex eternal object which does or might characterise it. So it is " a tale that might be told about actual entities."[1] The actual entities prehended, which might be described as the " food for a possibility," are the logical subjects; the eternal object, or more generally, complex eternal object is the predicate.

It is clear that by " logical subjects " Whitehead does not here mean the same as grammatical sub-

---

[1] *Process and Reality*, p. 362 (392).

jects, since (according to the view in his earlier
books) substantives in the grammatical sense
were shown to be adjectival, " objects," describing
the events, or actual occasions, comprising that
particular slice of the passage of nature.[1]   So in
the proposition " Socrates is mortal," the whole
verbal statement (" Socrates " included) would be
a complex eternal object describing that succession
of events which was the life history known as
Socrates.   But this does not mean that the proposition is to be analysed purely in terms of universals.   A proposition is a conceptual realisation
of a possibility as a form of definiteness characterising a set of actual entities in their definite nexus
with each other.   So the particular actual entities characterised in just that way are essential
to it.   Bradley's " Wolf-eating-lamb qualifying
the Absolute " leaves out the important question of
the way in which concrete particular fact enters
into a proposition.   A proposition is not a pure
potential.   It is a potentiality for fact, referring
to certain definite actual entities as its logical
subjects.   Whitehead says it might therefore be
described in Locke's words as an " idea determined
to particular existences."[2]   So every proposition
refers in some sense to particular existent actual
entities.   Those which do not are not propositions,

[1] Cf. *supra*, p. 109.
[2] *Process and Reality*, p. 279 (299).

but propositional functions. This is a notion very important for logic, but not sufficient when we want to assert anything about the actual world. A propositional function is a *form of a proposition*; that is to say, an expression containing one or more variables such that when values are assigned to them it becomes a proposition. So the *Principia Mathematica* is almost exclusively concerned with propositional functions; that is, with forms of propositions, such that when one form is asserted, other forms are seen to be implied in it. The usual symbol for a propositional function is $\phi(x)$, which means " any proposition $x$ of this form." (We thus meet the important notion of the *variable* —*e.g.* for *any* proposition of the form $p$ implies $q$, if $p$ is asserted, then $q$ is asserted.) Mathematics and mathematical logic show that if any proposition is of a certain form, certain other forms of propositions can be seen to be validly implied in it. But when we pass from propositional functions, which bring in the notion of the variable, and come to specific propositions, Whitehead claims that these must refer in some sense to the actual world. As soon as any definite value is assigned to $x$ the proposition refers to *some* actual entities as logical subjects and presupposes the actual world as exhibiting some sort of systematic character. This is called an " indicative system "[1] since the logical

[1] *Process and Reality*, pp. 274-276 (295-297).

subjects then become " Those particulars *as thus indicated* in such and such a predicative pattern." Every proposition presupposes the universe as exhibiting some systematic character which makes it " patient " of the fact asserted—we can see this if we try to analyse what we mean by saying " The whale is a mammal." So far, therefore, Whitehead would be in agreement with Bradley, who holds that every proposition ultimately implies the system of reality. But he avoids the familiar dilemma of monistic logic (which finds that this means we cannot say anything about anything without saying everything about everything) by holding that though every proposition presupposes *some* systematic aspect of the world, it does not presuppose the whole system of the world in all its detail. How this can be will be seen more clearly in the next chapter, where we shall see that certain systematic uniformities in the world are conceived as fundamental; others as belonging to special and limited types of order.

So Whitehead here diverges from Idealist logic mainly by insisting (*a*) that we must be able to say that *particulars* can be indicated in judgment; (*b*) that the fact that a proposition presupposes the world as exhibiting *some* systematic aspect does not mean that it implies the totality of the world in all its detail.

We may notice here that a distinction has crept

in between proposition and judgment. It is probably one of the most valuable contributions of Whitehead's view that he makes very clear wherein this distinction should be held to consist. He holds that a great deal of trouble has come from the fact that philosophers have treated propositions as though the primary thing about them was a logical judgment as to whether they were true or false.   But this is a late and highly sophisticated development.   Propositions primarily are not judged true or false but are *entertained*.   That is to say, they are what he describes as " lures for feeling," possibilities entertained by the subject (*i.e.* the subject which prehends, or " enjoys " them—not the logical subject) as relevant for realisation.   For instance, " redness of the book," " Hoover for President," " a drink of water " are types of proposition.   They may be (*a*) an urge after a difference, (*b*) something imagined as attractive or desirable, (*c*) a statement of the realisation of an eternal object in some actuality. Therefore, characteristically, Whitehead insists that propositional feelings are not restricted to conscious mentality.   They are the conceptual data of any feelings, *e.g.* of horror, indignation, desire, enjoyment etc.[1]   Consciousness arises from an integration of physical and conceptual feelings, when the conceptual feelings take the form of an

[1] Category of Explanation xviii.

affirmation-negation contrast—*e.g.* when I prehend something consciously as green, I am implicitly distinguishing it from the colours which it is not. (We may recall the statement in *Process and Reality*, I., ch. i., of the importance of the negative judgment in mentality.)

Propositions, therefore, may be broadly described as " lures for feeling." And so Whitehead makes what sounds like an almost immoral statement, that it is more important for a proposition to be interesting than for it to be true.[1] What he really means is that in some cases, the truth claim of a proposition adds to its interest and in others it does not. If for instance I say " An elephant is in this room," the proposition is trivial if false, but extremely interesting if true. If however we consider imaginative literature, which is throughout an example of complex propositions, the rôle of truth is not nearly so important. For instance, *Hamlet* is a very complex proposition. But we are not interested in whether it is true of its logical subjects, which were certain events in Denmark at a certain time. We are interested in it as a lure for enjoyment, or feeling.[2] On the

---

[1] *Process and Reality*, p. 366 (396).

[2] There is of course the wider sense, in which it is said that *Hamlet* is true " of human nature," or that it makes us understand the world better, and so forth. But the point is that this kind of " truth," whatever it may be (and this is a very difficult question), is quite clearly distinguishable from the truth

other hand, historical propositions derive their
interest from the fact that we believe these things
actually to have happened.   So the historian is
letting us down if his propositions are false.   The
whole interest in history lies in our believing that
it is an attempt at a propositional reconstruction of
things which really happened.

Note that truth and falsehood arise out of inte-
grations between the eternal objects as possibilities
and actual facts.   When there is an assertion of
such an integration on the part of a judging subject, we have a judgment.   A judgment may be
correct or incorrect; or if the integration is simply
asserted as possible, the judgment is suspended.[1]
Suspended judgments are of enormous importance
in science; and perhaps we may say also in
philosophy, since we do not have to commit
ourselves on all the theories we seek to understand, and assert as possible.   In fact, a large
part of this discussion of Whitehead's philo-

---

of the propositions in *Hamlet* about their logical subjects.   Perhaps we should say that " poetic truth," and possibly most of
what is called " religious truth," gives us insight, which makes
us appreciate the inner side of actuality called here " subjective
aim," rather than truth of propositions (*cf.* Chapter III.; and
A. D. Lindsay, *The Nature of Religious Truth* [London, 1927]).

[1] I take it that the distinction between a suspended judgment
and a proposition consists in the fact that the former brings in
the relation to a judging subject. See *Process and Reality*,
p. 271 (291).

8

sophy may be taken as a suspended judgment.

The essence of a judgment is a comparison of the nexus conceptually prehended with the nexus physically prehended, *i.e.* of the imagination of a possibility with the feeling of the compulsion of a "fact" (in the sense of a nexus of other actual entities). This of course depends again on the view of an actual entity as dipolar. Its physical pole is the feeling of other actual entities; its mental pole is the feeling of eternal objects, or the imaginative grasp of new possibilities. In the vast majority the latter is negligible, but its presence makes possible propositional feelings, and so the transition to higher forms of experience. Whitehead says that when we have an integration of the two kinds of feeling in the experiencing subject, we call the subjective form of its experience a judgment. If there is a complete comparison, so that the physical feeling and the conceptual feeling are seen exactly to fit, we have an intuitive judgment. But this is exceedingly rare, since there is hardly ever a conceptual feeling of a nexus of actual entities apart from abstraction and generalisation (in accordance with the Category of Transmutation).[1] So the vast

[1] *Cf.* Russell, *Analysis of Matter*, pp. 254-255, where it is shown that the difficulty of scientific inference lies in the fact that the relation S between percepts and a group of events constituting a physical object is nearly always many-one and not one-

majority of judgments are called " derivative." In this case we have only a partial comparison of the two nexūs. But when the abstraction and generalisation involved is clearly stated, the judgment may, within those limits, be correct or incorrect. For instance, I may judge correctly that the nexus of actual entities I call a left shoe will not fit with any degree of exactness on the nexus of actual entities I call a right foot.[1]

---

one, *e.g.* events may happen in the sun without being perceptible to us even with the best telescopes. So while exact similarity is a transitive relation, indistinguishability is not transitive. Russell gives the example of a heap of fine powder, which we may remove grain by grain, while at each stage there is no perceptible difference (*ibid.*, p. 282).

[1] How important it is to define the limits within which our judgment is correct was brought home to me by noticing, after I had written this, the point which Wittgenstein makes about almost this identical example (cf. *Tractatus* 6. 36111): " The Kantian problem of the right and left hand which cannot be made to cover one another already exists in the plane, and even in one-dimensional space; where the two congruent figures *a* and *b* cannot be made to cover one another without moving

$$- - o \; \frac{\quad\quad}{a} x - x \; \frac{\quad\quad}{b} \; o - - -$$

them out of this space. The right and left hand are in fact completely congruent. And the fact they cannot be made to cover one another has nothing to do with it.

" A right hand glove could be put on a left hand if it could be turned round in four-dimensional space."

So in four-dimensional space the White Knight and his Aged Aged Man may yet find their proper milieu.

We may illustrate this description of a judgment by means of a diagram.

Whitehead says[1] that his view can be looked on as either a coherence or a correspondence theory of truth. This is rather misleading, as he is not using either term in the sense in which we are accustomed to understand it in connection with theories of knowledge. He says his view is a "correspondence theory" of the truth and

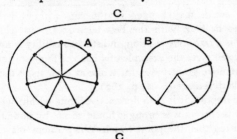

FIG. 3.

A=nexus physically prehended.
B=nexus conceptually prehended.
C=subjective form of judgment, in unity of experience of the judging subject.

falsehood of propositions, since it is concerned with a comparison between the complex eternal object considered as a possible predicate of a nexus of actual entities, and the actual qualities of that nexus. That is to say, the comparison is not between an idea in my head, and a fact (whatever

[1] *Process and Reality*, p. 270 (290).

such a comparison could conceivably mean), but between a form of definiteness symbolically represented, and one realised in the structure of the nexus. Both things compared are therefore in some sense actual, and truth and falsehood depend on a similarity in their structure. The view is also called a coherence theory of judgment, because in it the physical prehension of the nexus, and the conceptual prehension of the proposition are held together in the experience of the judging subject. If the experience is coherent, the judgment is correct. " Coherence " is therefore being taken to mean coherence of two different kinds of component within one experience. This seems an unfortunate use, in being different from what we customarily mean by coherence, *i.e.* the mutual implications of a system of propositions. I should therefore prefer to speak of Whitehead's theory of knowledge as a particular kind of correspondence theory.

Two further points may be noted. Since propositions refer to actualities of the actual world as their logical subjects, new propositions must be made possible by the creative advance of the world. So " Cæsar crossed the Rubicon " could not have been a proposition for Hannibal since the actual entities referred to in " Cæsar " were not then in existence.[1]

[1] *Ibid.*, p. 367 (396).

Secondly, a question arises as to whether there are what we may call " metaphysical propositions," *i.e.* propositions of complete generality, which would be true in all contexts for all judging subjects. These would relate simply to the general character of actualities, independently of the specific natures of particular events. Whitehead believes that there are metaphysical propositions, but doubts whether we can succeed in formulating them free from the empirical elements of our cosmic epoch.[1] He points to the mistakes which have been made in the past; for instance, the discovery of the limited applicability of Euclidean geometry.

$1 + 1 = 2$ looks like a metaphysical proposition; and Whitehead believes that he and Russell have proved it.[2] They defined exactly what is meant by 1, by 2 and by addition. Then we can say that one entity and another entity make two entities. But this is often put in the special form, which is not at all necessarily true, that if you

---

[1] He points out the distinction that must be made between metaphysics and cosmology. Metaphysics deals with the general nature of Being as such ; cosmology with the particular type of being of our world, and so brings in empirical elements. A cosmic epoch is a particular dominant type of world order ; for instance, our cosmic epoch is characterised by electro-magnetic occasions, with dimensions, shapes and measurability. But this may not be metaphysically necessary.

[2] *Principia Mathematica*, Prop. 110. 643.

have one *enduring object*, which is a succession
of entities (see the next chapter), and another, at
any time the two enduring objects will make two
separate societies of entities — *e.g.* a cup and
a saucer—viz.:

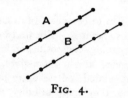

FIG. 4.

A and B are two separate enduring objects.
But why shouldn't they be like this ?

FIG. 5.

*i.e.* there be one occasion when they are identical ?
As a matter of fact, if actual entities are electro-
magnetic waves, this might quite well be so.

So we cannot be certain that we have formulated
any metaphysical proposition; though the underlying propositions of arithmetic (or the primitive propositions in the *Principia Mathematica*, or
something like them) seem to be fundamental,
at any rate for our epoch.

# CHAPTER VII

### CREATIVITY AND ORDER

To be is no other than to be one. In so far therefore as anything attains unity, in so far it is. For unity worketh congruity
and harmony, whereby things composite are, in so far as they are :
for things uncompounded are in themselves, because they are
one ; but things compounded imitate unity by the harmony of
their parts, and so far as they attain to unity, they are. Where-
fore order and rule secure being, disorder tends to not-being.—
St. Augustine.

We have now to consider the theory of prehensions
as a theory of the way in which actual entities
become organised into definite and recognisable
types of society. This is one aspect of what to
Whitehead is the central problem of metaphysics;
the relation between the permanent and fluent
elements of the world in a philosophy of process.
We have seen that in the context of the Philosophy of Organism the problem is set by the
holding together of two views; firstly, that the
ultimate constituents of nature are events (or
atomic actual occasions) which come to pass and
perish; and secondly, that *recognition*, involving
at any rate features in the passage of nature which
have some degree of permanence, is the essential
presupposition of any kind of observation, every

day no less than scientific. The problem set is, therefore, a form of the age-old problem seen by the Greeks; how it can be that the flux of nature exhibits characters which we can describe in terms of abstract universals, or, in other words, the problem of the forms in the facts. We must now see the bearing of this on the view that actual entities display different types of order.

It was noted above[1] that Whitehead remarks that one of the difficulties of an atomic cosmology is to explain how groups of actual entities can have common characteristics. The failure to do this means a failure to explain the apparent continuities and solidarities within nature. These must then just be looked on as aggregates of atoms, externally related. For if we consider an organic, or internal, type of relation, before we know where we are we have lost the self-subsistence and self-sufficiency of the atoms. So atomic philosophies have tended to look on growth and change as illusions—process is simply the combining together in different configurations of eternal and unchanging atoms. Even Leibniz' view of the development of the Monad by Appetition simply means an unfolding of its essential nature, from confused to clear perception. It is a simple substance, windowless, and cannot come into existence or perish by natural means. That

[1] See p. 158.

8*

is to say, it depends on a supernatural creation, and can only be destroyed by a supernatural annihilation.

But Whitehead is trying to run an atomic philosophy which will also be a philosophy of process. In doing so, we shall have to ask whether he is not putting forward a view incompatible with his organic view of the actual entity as a concrescence and also ask the relation of this to his former view of " objects and events." We shall have to ask whether he is not giving us two different descriptions, not altogether consistent with each other, of what constitutes a process of becoming.

In the first place, there is the view that actual entities are atomic.[1] He states that an actual entity as atomic comes into being, and perishes, but does not change. So he says[2] that Locke failed to see that " the doctrine of internal relations makes it impossible to attribute ' change ' to any actual entity. Every actual entity is what it is, with its definite status in the universe, determined by its internal relations to other actual entities.[3]

[1] *Process and Reality*, I., iii., § 3 and *passim*.

[2] *Ibid.*, p. 81 (92), and cf. *Principles of Natural Knowledge*, 14.3.

[3] It must be asked whether this is not a form of what Whitehead has called " the fallacy of simple location." Cf. *Science and the Modern World*, ch. iii. The statement that every actual entity is what it is with its definitely defined status in the universe

' Change ' is the description of the adventures of eternal objects in the evolving universe of actual things "; and " The fundamental meaning of the notion of change " is " the difference between actual occasions comprised in some determinate event."[1] Actual entities thus conceived come into being and perish; they are not instantaneous, for each is considered as comprising an atomic duration. This is called the " epochal theory of

---

has to be read in connection with the passages in *Science and the Modern World* in which the denial of simple location is stated in the sense that everything is to be thought of as pervading everything else. Russell (*Analysis of Matter,* p. 341) rightly says that such a view if taken seriously (and unguardedly stated) suggests a " mystic pantheism." But the initial statement of the meaning of " simple location " (*Science and the Modern World,* ch. iii., p. 69) shows that the " fallacy " lay in the ascription of an absolute position in Space and Time to a bit of matter without reference to other regions of Space and Time. Space and Time now become internal relations (*cf. ibid.,* p. 174) of events to each other. He therefore holds that the view of a definite status of a particular event, as defined by its internal relations to other events, is to be distinguished from the Newtonian view of its absolute position in Space and Time. But by holding to the private particularity (or " atomic character ") of an event, as well as saying that aspects of it are prehended by other events, he tries to state the principle of the organic solidarity of nature without simply ending in a " mystic pantheism." There are however serious difficulties in the passages where Whitehead states his " denial of simple location." These have been pointed out and discussed in detail by R. O. Lovejoy in *The Revolt against Dualism,* ch. v., pp. 156 *sq.* [1] *Process and Reality,* p. 101 (114).

time." An "epoch" (in the root sense of ἐποχή, an arrest or "hold up") is the slab of duration comprised by an atomic event. The epochal theory of time is connected with the view of an actual entity as vibratory, involving a period in which to realise itself. "This system, forming the primordial element, is nothing at any instant. It requires its whole period in which to manifest itself. In an analogous way, a note of music is nothing at an instant, but it also requires its whole period in which to manifest itself."[1] That is to say, the event is a unity, but one in which earlier and later incomplete phases may be distinguished, so that it is said to involve a duration. But neither motion nor change can be attributed to the processes of concrescence as wholes. They are what they are; they happen and perish. They are described in terms of the theory of feelings as "throbs of emotion"; in terms of physical science, they may be quantum vibrations.[2] What we call

[1] *Science and the Modern World*, p. 52.

[2] See *Ibid.*, ch. viii. It is clear from this chapter that Whitehead's particular view of actual occasions is in no way bound up with the Quantum Theory, the exact interpretation of which is still problematic. But if that theory be true, his view of actual entities gains a certain amount of empirical application; while he is simply concerned to point out that "the cosmological outlook, which is here adopted, is perfectly consistent with the demands for discontinuity which have been urged from the side of physics" (*loc. cit.*, p. 192).

change and permanence, motion and rest are variations and reiterations of the pattern formed by successive atomic occasions. So what is permanent throughout a succession of actual occasions is the *form*. The form is an eternal object, which is situated, or ingredient in a route of successive events.[1]  In *The Concept of Nature*, the continuity of nature was stated to be a continuity of events, while its recognisable characters were called " objects."[2]  Objects are characters of nature of which we can say they can " be again," whereas events are fluent and continuous.

An event has the fundamental property of extensiveness over other events; and the events it extends over are called its parts.[3]  Thus events are conceived as having parts, namely the other events over which they extend; and in Whitehead's earlier discussions, all the relations of an event which are interpreted in terms of the fundamental property of extensiveness are conceived in terms of the notion of whole and part. Now, however,[4] the relation of whole and part is taken as a more limited notion to be derived from the general notion of extensive connection. But extensive connection is still the primary and

---

[1] Cf. *Concept of Nature*, ch. vii.
[2] *Ibid.*, p. 144.
[3] *Principles of Natural Knowledge*, 15. 7, 18. 4.
[4] *Process and Reality*, p. 407 (439–440).

fundamental relation between actual occasions.[1] How is this compatible with the notion of actual occasions as atomic ?

We may now revert to the second description of the nature of an actual occasion—namely, as a concrescence, or prehending thing. At first sight we might say that this is an entirely different notion from that of actual occasions as atomic and perishing, but displaying a structure of repeated patterns, to be described in terms of eternal objects. If the actual entity is a concrescence, it undergoes at any rate internal development : if this is all we mean by " change," the actual entity is as windowless as Leibniz' monad; but if this development is the result of its prehensions of the rest of the world, we should say that we have a description of an organic process of growth which cannot be described in terms of atomism. The word " atomism " is an unfortunate one for Whitehead to have used, since it has the connotation of ultimate and enduring particles, in external relation to one another. What he wishes to bring out is presumably that

---

[1] *Process and Reality*, p. 408 (441). It is perhaps unnecessary to point out that " extensive connection " does not necessarily mean the same as " spatial " connection, which is a more special notion. It is the general character of relatedness, which we shall discuss presently when we come to the " Extensive Continuum " ; and it may be described in terms of the notions of " overlapping," " contact," and " whole and part."

an actual entity is an individualised activity; he is therefore in search of a Monadology rather than an atomism. Indeed, if we can substitute " feeling " for perception, or understand by perception a form of feeling with a " vector " reference to what is perceived, we might well say in Leibnizian language that an actual entity perceives the whole universe from its point of view. But since an actual entity is not a substance supporting qualities, but an individualised feeling, it has no permanence. Its feeling is its whole nature, in which it becomes and perishes. The feeling ought not to be called atomic, if this implies that it has no parts, since its comprising a duration means that there are earlier and later phases of the concrescence and these are to be considered as extending over other events. But presumably Whitehead now speaks of events as atomic in order to bring out his view that these phases only have meaning in terms of the final satisfaction of the concrescence as a whole. This is stated in Categorical Obligations i.-iii., and Category of Explanation xxviii. The precise meaning of the matter may be made clearer by means of a diagram. (See page 182.)

A and B, are phases in the concrescence of an actual entity. C is the final phase, not yet reached. D is another actual entity, prehended positively by A. There is therefore a new prehension of D by B, *via* A, *i.e.* B prehends A-as-prehending-D, and so also the subjective form of A's prehension of D.   E is, say, an eternal object negatively prehended by A.   B therefore prehends A-as-negatively-prehending-E, and hence the subjective form of A's negative prehension of E, but not E itself.   *xy* is a cut at an incomplete phase in the concrescence.   At this cut, the prehensions will be incomplete and unintegrated.[1]   But since

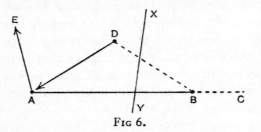

FIG 6.

a process of concrescence occupies a certain duration, in which earlier and later phases can be distinguished, these are integrated into one another in the whole concrescence.

If we are justified in finding a difficulty in reconciling this with the view of actual occasions as atomic and perishing, the root of it lies in the fact that Whitehead does not state as clearly as we might wish the relation between the individual concrescent occasion, and the nexus of occasions which forms a " thing," or " organism " in the

[1] Categorical Obligation i.

usual sense, namely of a structured whole of parts organised for a certain end. Any natural thing which we can imagine, however small, is to be described as a nexus of actual occasions. Since actual occasions themselves do not move or change, but are perpetually perishing, anything that permits of recognition and movement must be a complex nexus.[1] The term "event" used in Whitehead's earlier books as a final fact of nature, and so corresponding to what we would now take him to mean by actual occasion, is here[2] said to be a nexus of actual occasions (such for instance as a molecule) "interrelated in some determinate fashion in one extensive quantum." Our difficulty, of how events are to have parts which are the other events over which they extend, can only be resolved if we take the "event" of the earlier books to be a complex of what he describes in *Process and Reality* as "actual occasions."

But a difficulty still remains in conceiving the atomic occasion, even if it be a process of becoming, as enjoying a "subjective aim," "propositional feelings," and the other kinds of prehension of the rest of its world, involving subtle appreciation of the "contrasts" which it might stage. To put it crudely and bluntly, a "throb of emotion" occupying about the dimensions of a quantum

[1] *Process and Reality*, p. 101 (113-114).
[2] *Ibid.*, p. 101 (113).

vibration would not have time to live such an interesting life.[1] Are not all these descriptions of the kinds of prehension involved in a concrescence applicable rather to the nexus of actual entities as a whole, taken over a long spell in its history ? We can with some plausibility talk of an animal as having a subjective aim; but can we seriously use the same language of an " electronic occasion " ?

The only way we can answer this sort of difficulty, which must naturally arise in the minds of a good many of Whitehead's readers, is by taking up his suggestion[2] that the Philosophy of Organism is a " cell " theory of actuality;[3] and especially

---

[1] *Cf.* Professor Lloyd Morgan's " Subjective Aim in Whitehead's Philosophy " in the *Journal of Philosophical Studies*, July, 1931.

[2] *Process and Reality*, Pt. III., i., § 1.

[3] *Cf.* J. H. Woodger, *Biological Principles*, pp. 294 *sq.* Woodger points out (p. 493) that the word " cell " is commonly used to cover three different meanings : (i.) a certain type of biological organisation, (ii.) the events having this type of organisation, (iii.) the visual perceptual object which may be seen through the microscope. He himself decides to restrict the term to meaning (i.), and apply it to the type of organisation which proceeds through spatial repetition by division. Whitehead's application of the term " cell-theory " is clearly wider than this, though it would include it. But it is consonant with the fundamental point in the cell-theory, which Woodger states to be the fact that this type of organisation characterises *parts* of organisms whose organisation is above this level; and " parts

by following the valuable guidance of *Science and the Modern World*, ch. v., pp. 109-112. He there shows the problem of materialism in explaining the evolution of a thing like the human body-mind, if it is simply made up of molecules which " blindly run " according to mechanical laws.    In the Philosophy of Organism, on the other hand, he says: " The concrete enduring entities are organisms, so that the plan of the *whole* influences the very characters of the various subordinate organisms which enter into it.    In the case of an animal, the mental states enter into the plan of the total organism and thus modify the plans of the successive subordinate organisms until the ultimate smallest organisms, such as electrons, are reached.    Thus an electron within a living body is different from an electron outside it, by reason of the plan of the body.    The electron blindly runs either within or without the body; but it runs within the body in accordance with its character within the body. . . ." It is this plan of the whole which we naturally want to describe in terms of subjective aim, " grasp at novelty," and so forth, whereas it sounds unnatural to apply these terms to the individual atomic occasions.    Yet we must consider care-

---

of one organism are organically related, and this relation is such that the parts behave differently *in* this relation from what they do out of it " (*op. cit.*, pp. 310-311).

fully, in the light of the Ontological Principle and the concept of process, in what sense we can talk of there being a " plan of the organism as a whole," as distinguished from its component actual entities. He reminds us that all the life of the body is in its millions of individual cells; there is no " life of the whole " as an entelechy over and above this. But there is co-ordinated and organised activity, so that a plan of the body as a whole is served by this particular type of organisation of its millions of centres of life. So if we are to try to formulate a thoroughgoing organic theory of nature something like this view of the integrated subjective aims of the individual actual occasions will be necessary; and the apparent pathetic fallacy or anthropomorphisms it at present involves may be due to the difficulties of expressing these things in a language which is not misleading.

In the first place, let us revert to the statement that actual entities are atomic and perish subjectively, so that what is permanent throughout a succession of actual entities is the *form*. What reason is there for a route of actual entities, if they are simply atomic and perishing, to reproduce the same form, so that we may recognise the route, and call it an " enduring object," such as a stone, or a leaf, or a man's life? Still more, what could be the reason for the stability of types of society of actual entity in the reproduction of species?

According to the doctrine of the objectification of one actual entity into another which feels it as a stubborn fact, each actual entity as it perishes will be felt by the one immediately supervening. So its character will be reproduced by reason of a peculiarly close conformity of feeling. We thus have the inheritance of a common form through the prehension of the preceding members by each member of the nexus as it arises. . . . . . . . -> A series of actual entities of this kind is called a "strand," or enduring object. Ordinary physical objects and "bodies" are such strands. We have the inheritance of a common form through a historic route of occasions.[1] If we interpret "form" in the Aristotelian sense, as meaning a certain type of structure organised for a certain end, we may notice an almost exact forecast of this view in Locke's section[2] on the Identity of Vegetables, which discusses how it is that a succession of fleeting particles of matter can be said to form the same tree. "That being then one plant which has such an organisation of parts in one coherent body, partaking of one common

[1] *Cf.* Russell, *Analysis of Matter*, p. 81, where a "material object" is described as a certain qualitative continuity in a string of events. [2] *Essay*, Bk. II., xxvii., 4.

life, it continues to be the same plant as long as it partakes of the same life, though that life be communicated to new particles of matter vitally united to the living plant in a like continued organisation, conformable to that sort of plants." But this " partaking of the same life," if we do not look on the " life " or the formal structure as a mysterious something over and above the succession of actual entities (and to do so would break the Ontological Principle), we must say consists in the reproduction in the living immediacy of the present actual entities of the character of the actual entities of the immediate past, which they felt as they arose, and so objectified in themselves.   This is the sense in which we should take the statement[1] that " relatedness is wholly concerned with the appropriation of the dead by the living."   So a nexus in the past with peculiar relevance to us may be called " our " past.   I am an historic route of occasions culminating in the contemporary me.   Such a route of historic occasions is said to have serial or personal order. The point about this type of order is that each occasion inherits the dominating characteristic of the occasions on one side of it.   Thus in the following diagram[2] A and B both inherit from the occasions on the left side of the cut *xy* in the strand, but from none on the right.

[1] *Process and Reality*, p. viii (ix).          [2] See Fig. 7.

The " enduring object " as a whole can then be said to sustain a character (the primary meaning of " person "). This character is inherited throughout the whole of an historic route of occasions. (So, as Whitehead pleasantly puts it, we may define a " person " as one who inherits the wealth of all his relations.) But the notion of serial or personal order is extremely general, and nexūs with this kind of personal order may of course be more and less complex. A simple type

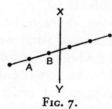

FIG. 7.

of personal order is a single strand or " enduring object." But a complex type, such as any physical body, is a society of many such strands. If the nexus has what is called " social " order, each occasion in each strand inherits some of the dominating characteristics of the society, so that it can be said that the society as a whole sustains a character. If the society can be analysed into strands of enduring objects which have their own defining characteristics, the society is called " corpuscular." A society may be more or less corpuscular, according to the relative importance of the defining characteristics of the strands which make it up, and of the nexus as a whole.

The problem of repetition then becomes that of the inheritance by one actual entity of the character of another, and this, according to the Ontological Principle, can only be by the objectifying of one actual entity into another by " feeling." We have to speak therefore at any rate to this extent of every actual entity as enjoying feeling and a subjective aim, if it be only that of conformity and reproduction.

But the common characteristic of a nexus of actual entities, and so of what we called the plan of the society as a whole, depends upon the type of " order " which the actual entities composing it form. The concept of order is of course a fundamental one in mathematics, and it is probably its mathematical sense which Whitehead has in mind. Broadly speaking, this may be defined as a set of terms arranged in a certain way, so that the meaning of any term depends on its place in the series. So in the series of integers, which is a certain type of order, 0 has a different significance in 10, and in 1,000, and in ·01. There are a large number of different ways of arranging any finite number of things according to their permutations and combinations, but there is generally one way which is important for a particular purpose, and yields a particular result

So when we say that a nexus of actual entities exhibits a type of order, we mean that the actual entities are arranged and organised in a certain way so that the whole is not a mere aggregate, but has a unified structure which gives it an interest as a whole; and that this depends on the many actual entities being interwoven by their prehensions of one another in just *that* way.[1] A forest therefore displays a type of order, so does a gas, or a stone, or a government, or a man's life.

A prejudice against speaking of "order" in this connection is due to our thinking that by "order" is meant something dull and tidy, out of which all life and spontaneity and creativeness has gone. Perhaps the word "pattern", which

[1] Since all apprehension implies selection, and so abstraction from a vaguely felt totality, those systematic relations of which we are aware in a complex of fact are simply those which for certain purposes it is important for us to notice (all attention, as W. James pointed out, depending on interest). But innumerable other types of relation may be being exemplified in the same complex. So Whitehead has made the interesting suggestion that all the different kinds of geometry may be exemplified in the physical universe, although for our purposes we are most constantly aware of the Euclidean relational order.

*Cf.* Russell, *Analysis of Matter*, pp. 5-6. "It is of course possible and even likely, that various different geometries, which would be incompatible if applied to the same set of objects, may all be applicable to the empirical world by means of different interpretations."

is fashionable just now in philosophy and psychology, helps to strengthen this prejudice. A pattern immediately suggests a static and dead morphology. Yet the true alternative to order is not creative life, or art, but chaos. So, Whitehead repeatedly insists, mere unbounded creativity can produce nothing. Actuality is always a limitation on pure creativity; and as soon as you have limitation, you have decision between alternatives, which means some kind of definite ordering. As the Pythagoreans saw long ago, the Limit is essential to Being. We may refer to the quotation from St. Augustine at the beginning of this chapter, where, in the spirit of Greek philosophy, he reminds us that "in so far as things attain to unity, they are." Any reflection on the beauty of form in art should assure us that order does not mean something dead and unimaginative. That fascinating study of "the ways of the imagination," John Livingstone Lowes' *The Road to Xanadu* brings this out very clearly, in words which exactly express in literary what Whitehead is saying in philosophical language. "For the Road to Xanadu . . . is the road of the human spirit, and the imagination voyaging through chaos and reducing it to clarity and order is the symbol of all the quests which lend glory to our dust. And the goal of the shaping spirit which hovers in the *poet's* brain is the clarity and order of pure beauty. Nothing is alien to its transforming touch. . . . Yet the pieces that compose the pattern are not new. In the world of the shaping spirit, save for its patterns, there is nothing new that was not old. For the work of the creators is the mastery, transmutation and reordering into shapes of beauty of the given universe within us and without us. The shapes thus wrought are not that universe; they are 'carved with figures strange and sweet, All made out of the carver's brain.' Yet in that brain the elements and shattered fragments of the figures already lie, and what the carver-creator sees, implicit in the fragments, is the unique and lovely Form."

Here again a misunderstanding or objection may be raised against such a use of the concept of " order." It may be said that such language implies the perception of a form or pattern, which we may perhaps even conceive as " laid up in heaven," which is then expressed in the given material, which is plastic in the hands of the artist creator. Whereas is not the truth, in creative living no less than in creative art, that we have a blind urge which is not clearly understood until it has found expression ? In Professor Alexander's words, " Just as the object known is revealed through the ordinary reaction to it; so the work of art is revealed to the artist himself through the productive act wrung from him in his excitement over the subject-matter. Accordingly, he does not in general first form an image (if he is a poet, say) of what he wants to express, but finds out what he wanted to express by expressing it; he has, in general, no precedent image of his work, and does not know what he will say till he has said it, and it comes as a revelation to himself."[1] But it may be pointed out that even so, if anything has been expressed, on looking back at it, it will be seen that a form, an order has shaped itself, though it may be one that the artist could not possibly have foreseen. There is a so-called " inevitability " about a work of art —a play, for instance, or a symphony—which is not inconsistent with its being unpredictable.

Whitehead puts this point of view in his discussion of what he calls the " satisfaction " of an actual entity, and of a process of becoming as the transformation of incoherence into coherence. The summary statement of this will be found in the first three Categorical Obligations, and the 26th and 27th Categories of Explanation. They variously state that a complete understanding of the nature of an actual entity must wait until it has fully become. Then each partial phase in its process of becoming will be seen as contributing to the total result, in which each

[1] *Artistic and Cosmic Creation.* Annual Philosophical Lecture to the British Academy, 1927.

plays its own part, and no element is simply duplicated. So the final phase of the actual entity, when it has "achieved definiteness" shows its own reason for what it includes and what it omits. This can be illustrated by a picture. When it is complete, no line or feature could be added without upsetting the balance of the whole and making it no longer *that* picture. Similarly, Whitehead says, a concrescence must terminate in "one determinate integral satisfaction."

It may be suggested that we here have simply an echo of Idealist Logic, of the view of the real as the self-consistent individual. And in fact Whitehead makes the statement that "Logic is the general analysis of self-consistency,"[1] *i.e.* the analysis of the factors in a "satisfaction" (the process called "co-ordinate division"). But there is a distinction. The Idealist view looks on the real as the self-consistent system of thought, so that the consistency of actuality is the same as logical consistency. Whitehead, on the other hand, is starting from the end not of logic but of the becoming actuality. Consistency is something to be achieved when the actuality has fully become, and is not there all along for thought to understand.[2] But when the actuality has

[1] *Process and Reality*, p. 35 (39).
[2] This is underlined by the fact that Whitehead holds that there is a type of existence which he calls a "multiplicity,"

become, it is self-consistent in the sense that an understanding of it shows the reason for what it includes and what it excludes. Each part then contributes its full quota to the whole—it might be described as an ἐνεργεῖα ἀνεῦ δυνάμεως, a completely determinate activity. A good statement of what is meant by the rational consistency of the real in this sense is made by Professor N. Kemp Smith.[1] " Under the conditions prescribed, a rationality or order appropriate to them, discloses itself; an order which is richer and more wonderful than any unassisted, that is dialectical reasoning could ever have anticipated, if called on to invent what it would desire to discover. It is for the universe on detailed study to reveal the kind of rationality which does in fact belong to it. . . . What the rationalist can alone be required to stand for is the conviction that reality if known in all its details and all its manifold aspects will be found to justify itself in face of the claims to which it has given rise in *any* of its embodiments."[2]

---

which is described as a group of diverse entities given in disjunction. An example is the actual world from which a concrescence arises, regarded as an initial datum which has not yet been brought into a unity of prehension.

[1] *University of California Publications in Philosophy*, vol. iii.

[2] *Cf.* A. E. Taylor, *The Faith of a Moralist*, ii., p. 92, and especially his quotation from Sir Walter Raleigh's *Shakespeare*

Reality might thus be defined as the final justification of experience.[1]  This again suggests Absolute Idealism; but it should be noted that the Philosophy of Organism is an attempt to apply this principle to a pluralistic universe.  In Absolute Idealism, the Absolute may be its own reason for what it is, but it is the only actual entity.

Moreover, Whitehead would agree with Leibniz, that self-consistent thought gives only the possible, whereas actuality is a "decision" among possibilities, which therefore contains, as stubborn fact, an element of "givenness" the sufficient reason for which cannot be found by logical analysis alone.  We may note that logical analysis of the actual entity is only possible when it has become, and is "objectively immortal"; and even thus the sufficient reason for its being that particular process of self-formation is only to be found in its subjective aim, which, he says, is grasped not by analysis but by intuition (in the Bergsonian sense).

We may refer in this connection to the 9th Categorical Obligation, which states that the

[1] A greater difficulty here, if we are to take process seriously, is our doubt as to whether things *do* achieve definiteness and coherence.  We seem to see everywhere stunted, broken and incoherent growth.  What may be said of this must wait to the last chapters.

concrescence of each individual actual entity is internally determined and externally free. This internal determination is Professor Alexander's definition of freedom as " determination as enjoyed." The nature of an actual entity cannot be fully predicted or understood from an analysis of its prehensions (so it is " externally free "); in analysing them " whatever is determinable is determined," but the final sufficient reason for the actual entity being what it is depends on its " decision," on the kick of emphasis, by emotion, appreciation, or purpose, which it gives its prehensions, and this is determined by its internal subjective aim. Hence the insistent feeling of the responsibility of an actual entity for being what it is. This is illustrated from the course of history.[1] On looking back on it, we can see how one part leads out of another, and speak of it as internally determined. Yet no sufficient reason can be given externally to itself as to why it should have been *that* course of events rather than any other. We might venture on a similar speculation about the history of thought. In studying the history of thought, we see how certain questions were raised by the Greeks, and then how they led on to the kind of philosophical speculation we find in mediæval, renaissance, and modern times. So there is a certain internal

---

[1] *Process and Reality*, p. 64 (74).

determination of the dialectic of the history of thought. But supposing quite other questions had been raised—suppose for instance the concept of Substance had never been formed—might not our whole categories of thought, and the kind of discussion we indulge in, have been quite diffferent?

Let us turn now to the way in which Whitehead says cosmic creation is to be conceived, as the arising of definite types of order. In the first place we must bear in mind his insistence that sheer, blind creativity and unbounded potentiality between them could produce nothing. There would be no sufficient reason for *any* course of creation whatsoever. Therefore, like Leibniz, Whitehead holds that if we are to say that the realm of possibility is wider than the realm of actuality (as we must, if we are to avoid Spinoza's determinism), we must say that there must be a primordial limitation on pure creativity in virtue of which there is a sufficient reason for *some* (though, unlike Leibniz, Whitehead would not say for this specific) actual course of events. This is the sense in which God is said to be the Principle of Concretion. Secondly, according to the Ontological Principle, the reason for this limitation is to be found in the nature of an actual entity. So, he argues, there must be a primordial created fact, which is a limitation on pure creativity. The theological and religious implications of this will

9

be taken up and discussed in Chapter IX. All that we can do here is to note that the nature of this first limitation upon creativity will constitute the conditions laid upon any other process of becoming whatsoever, since, according to the doctrine of objective immortality, when it has become, it will be a stubborn fact for all other actualities. This is the sense in which we are to understand the statement that metaphysical principles are truths about the Primordial Nature of God. Since, according to the Ontological Principle, there can be no " laws " or " order " of nature apart from the characteristics of actual entities, when we wish to say anything about principles of complete generality, we must find the reasons for them in the Primordial Nature of God. This, then, is to be considered as the general character of order imposed on any course of creation whatsoever. Within the bounds of this, we come to other conditions of relatedness between actual entities. It must be remembered that actual entities are atomic, " decisions " amid potentiality. But if atomic actual entities are to display the types of stabilised structure which alone make possible the repetition and contrast which are essential for recognition (and so the condition of all science and observation), he holds that they must display certain systematic uniformities. This uniform scheme of relations is called

the Extensive Continuum.  It may be asked
wherein it differs from the Primordial Nature of
God, since if it were a systematic relatedness of
potentialities apart from the nature of some actual
entity, we should have a breach of the Ontological
Principle.  The answer must be that its generality, though complete for the temporal world, is
not as complete as that of the Primordial Nature
of God, which holds for all possible worlds.  So[1]
the Extensive Continuum " is not a fact prior to the
world; it is the first determination of order—that
is, of real potentiality—arising out of the general
character of the world."  That is to say, it is the
general scheme of relatedness displayed by the
actual entities of all cosmic epochs of the world.
Whitehead suggests that its properties are the
relations of whole and part, overlapping and
contact; whereas the relations of metrical geometry,
shapes, dimension and measurability, may not
extend beyond our cosmic epoch.

This means that he has to defend a view that
the most general type of relation between events
is that alluded to at the beginning of this chapter
—namely, their property of extending over other
events; a relation  called " extensive connection,"
in terms of which the more limited notion of
" whole and part " can now be defined.[2]

---

[1] *Process and Reality*, p. 92 (103).
[2] *Process and Reality*, pp. 408-409 (440-442).

So we start from a view of nature as exclusively made up of events, or nexūs of actual entities (whichever terminology we prefer);[1] and say that one event has the property of extending over other events.   Thus the event which is all nature during a minute extends over the event which is all nature during 30 seconds; or, if we wish to avoid bringing in the notion of a duration, we can say that one event extends over another when every region (*i.e.* event which is a relatum of extensive connection) included in region B is also connected with region A.   Region B may then be called " part " of region A.[2]

Therefore, starting from events and their

---

[1] In the description of the passage of nature as a " continuum of events " an " event " would have to be taken, in the light of his present view of atomic actual entities, as a nexus of actual entities, which can overlap others and so be extensively connected with them.

[2] *Process and Reality*, Pt. IV., ch. ii., p. 419 (452).   It is impossible here to go into the very interesting developments of the notion of extensive connection which Whitehead makes in this chapter, as a result of adopting Professor de Laguna's suggestion of the substitution of the notion of extensive connection for that of extensive whole and extensive part.   It enables him to define the notions of mediate connection, overlapping, external and tangential connection, as well as the example I have selected of " inclusion," in terms of extensive connection.   In spite of a very insufficient grasp of the notions involved, I can see that this chapter is one of the most valuable, and likely to be one of the most permanently satisfactory, in *Process and Reality*.

property of extensive connection, Whitehead has to show how their other systematic uniformities can be derived from this, and particularly those uniformities called spatial and temporal relations. This he does by his famous Method of Extensive Abstraction. It will not be possible to discuss this in any detail; a full exposition is to be found in the *Principles of Natural Knowledge*, and *The Concept of Nature*, chs. iii. and iv.; and a clear shorter exposition of the fundamental principle involved, in his *Aims of Education*, ch. ix. ("The Anatomy of Some Scientific Ideas").[1]

Briefly, we may say that the Method of Extensive Abstraction is a description of the way in which we may search for the "forms in the facts"; that is to say, how, starting from concrete events, we may find that they display systematic characters which can be expressed in terms of universals. So we can look on space and time not as a framework within which events take place, but as uniform relations displayed by concrete events in their "passage." Then what do we mean by instants of time and points in space ? A concrete event is all nature throughout a certain duration. This may be conceived as extending over the event which is nature throughout a shorter duration, and this over another event, and so on. Such a

[1] *The Aims of Education and Other Essays*, pp. 205 *sq.* (London, 1929).

series of events with temporal extension may be conceived as covering each other, like a nest of Chinese boxes packed one inside the other. The series we might say converges not to a smallest box, but to an ideal limit, which would be nature without temporal extension, *i.e.* at an instant of time. But Whitehead says that to call the point or the instant the " ideal limit " of the converging abstractive set is really meaningless. It is not the proper meaning of " limit " in a mathematical series; in fact an " ideal limit " is really nothing at all. To call it a fiction is no better, since he holds that " fiction " is simply an ambiguous term which fails to say whether there is any important fact or relation in nature to which what are called points and instants correspond. Here he is conservative, compared with modern mathematicians, like Poincaré for instance, who are perfectly content with the notion of fictions. Whitehead continually, as we have seen, insists that science and mathematics must be saying something important about some actual or possible systematic connection within nature, or they are a mere day-dream. So if the elements we call points are not the " ideal limits " of the converging abstractive sets, we must say they are the *route of convergence* of the whole set. A geometrical element, such as a point, is therefore defined as the " group of routes of approximation to a definite intrinsic character of ideal simplicity, to be found as a limit among natural facts."[1] The important point to notice is that the element itself is *the whole class of abstractive sets* with the same convergent

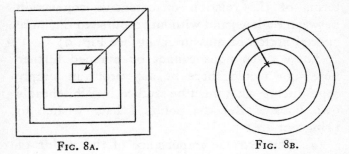

Fig. 8A.　　　　　Fig. 8B.

character. So a point is defined both by the set in Fig. 8A, and by the set in Fig. 8B.

The discussions of the different kinds of abstractive sets, and their relations to each other,

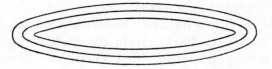

Fig. 9.

defining the different abstractive elements is of extreme interest. It is to be found in the passages referred to in the *Principles of Natural Knowledge*, and *The Concept of Nature* ; and Whitehead's

[1] *Concept of Nature*, p. 84.

latest developments of it are to be found in *Process and Reality*, Pt. IV.   Perhaps the most interesting of these is the definition of a straight line in terms of an abstractive set of ovals, and so purely in terms of the relation of extensive connection between regions, and without recourse to the more special notion of measurement (see Fig. 9).

These discussions cannot be pursued further here, nor would there be any profit in simply reproducing what must be studied in Whitehead's own books.   But the points I have wished to bring out are:

(*a*) The extreme importance of the notion of extensive connection for the Philosophy of Organism.   It enables him to hold to the Ontological Principle, and yet to express the most complex mathematical notions in terms of abstractions arrived at from systematic relations between actual entities in a nexus.

(*b*) That this implies a relational view of space and time, as deducible from the mutual relations of diverse processes of becoming.[1]   Uniform space and time are arrived at by a method of abstraction from the relations between concrete events, occupying " slabs of duration,"[2] and involving their own spatial and temporal systems.

---

[1] See the essay " Space, Time and Relativity " at the end of the *Aims of Education* (especially p. 244).

[2] Cf. *supra* p. 178.

(c) That this appeal to a systematic uniformity expressible in the relations of the Extensive Continuum is, Whitehead holds, essential if there is to be any justification of scientific generalisation, *i.e.* of Induction, or of measurement.

Induction demands an analogy between things which have been observed, and things not observed. If we are to assume that the evidence we have got about nature can in any respect point the same way as the evidence we have not got, we must appeal to some systematic characters common to both the facts known and those unknown. We may compare Mr. Keynes' " Principle of the Limitation of Variety." The justification of Induction, he says,[1] depends on the assumption " that the objects in the field, over which our generalisations extend, do not have an infinite number of independent qualities, that, in other words, their characteristics, however numerous, cohere together in groups of invariable connection which are finite in number."

That is the basis of Whitehead's contention that all Induction is statistical. If statistical generalisation is to be of any value in forecasting— *e.g.* if from the number of births in a country over a period of years we can estimate the probable number next year—we must be able to appeal to a stability of the general conditions of the en-

[1] *A Treatise on Probability* (London, 1921), p. 256.

9*

vironment; and to certain conditions as relevant, and others as irrelevant, to the statistical generalisation. So he holds that a metaphysic which exhibits the universe as systematic, and also as dissectible into partial systems with degrees of mutual relevance, is essential to the justification of Induction. And a similar assumption is necessary for the justification of measurement, which is fundamental to science. Whitehead shows that measurement depends upon Congruence—*i.e.* upon the judgment of an identity of function within a systematic complex of relations. Even if we allow that scientific measurement is only approximate, the notion of an ideal exactness to which it approximates presupposes that our instruments will remain to a certain extent constant when transferred from one thing to another; that one inch along the length of a measuring rod will perform a similar function to the next inch. We may be told that developments of the theory of relativity, the hypothesis of the FitzGerald contractions, and so on, make all this appeal to systematic uniformities in nature, implied in measurement of the physical field, unduly conservative. But it may be observed that even distortions such as the FitzGerald contractions are supposed to have a certain systematic regularity about them.

Whitehead contends that unless there be uniformities underlying our actual fragmentary experiences they could not " sustain that connected infinite world in which in our thoughts we live."[1] Here again, we may say, he is making the old assumption which Kant challenged, that what is a necessity for thought is also a necessity for things. Miss Stebbing, in her paper " Mind and Nature in Professor Whitehead's Philosophy "[2] pointed out the anomaly in Whitehead's using an argument from " the necessity for knowledge that there be a system of uniform relatedness "[3] in a *Naturphilosophie* which, at that time, definitely held that Nature was closed to mind. Now that Whitehead includes epistemology in his wider metaphysic, such an argument is less anomalous. But does it really help much, beyond showing that the justification of Induction and measurement, and the assumption of a systematic uniformity in nature, stand and fall together ?[4] He can however very plausibly urge that an appeal to a dominant and uniform space-time continuum is implied in our distinction of veridical from dream, or illusory, experience; and even implied by Hume,

[1] " Space, Time and Relativity," in the *Aims of Education*, p. 246.  [2] *Mind*, July, 1924.

[3] See *Principle of Relativity*, p. 29.

[4] So Russell remarks (*The Analysis of Matter*, p. 79), " Dr. Whitehead's view seems to rest upon the assumption that the principles of scientific inference ought in some way to be ' reasonable.' " Russell does not consider this a sufficient ground for rejecting Einstein's geometry of a variable space.

when he speaks of " the connection of contiguity in time and place."[1]

He might also answer that, if he appeals to an assumption of " the uniformity of the texture of experience," at any rate he does so openly, and claims that, as in any case we *do* have measurement and observation, and scientific reasoning by Induction and Analogy, we may as well own openly the metaphysic which a justification of this implies.[2] And if the assumption be false, we must give up the hope that science can ever aim to afford

> " a support
> Not treacherous to the mind's *excursive* power."

We must now return to his view of what is implied in the more special concept of the order of nature. Again, in accordance with the Ontological Principle, there can be no " laws of nature " externally imposing order on actual entities. The reason for the laws must be found in the character of actual entities. So within the general system of the metaphysical conditions found in the Primordial Nature of God, and of the relatedness

[1] *Cf.* Whitehead's the Presidential Address to the Aristotelian Society (1922), " Uniformity and Contingency," *Proceedings of the Aristotelian Society*, vol. xxiii., especially pp. 6-8.

[2] Cf. *Aims of Education*, p. 246. " The fact that immediate experience is capable of this deductive superstructure must mean that it itself has a certain uniformity of texture."

of the world found in the character of the Extensive Continuum, we have what are called " laws of nature," as descriptions of the dominant characteristics of wide societies of actual entities. Such types of societies of actual entities may arise and decay, and so we get what Whitehead calls different " cosmic epochs," or dominant types of cosmic order. Our cosmic epoch is characterised by star-systems, and electro-magnetic events, but this may not be metaphysically necessary.

Within a cosmic epoch we also get the arising and decaying of countless more special types of order. This view clearly does not regard what is loosely called the process of evolution as single and unilateral. Nor does it support the notion of a " progress " towards " one far-off divine event To which the whole creation moves," as it were *en bloc*. Instead, we have to conceive of the creative process as the gradual building up and decaying of innumerable types of order. Spengler's morphology of history suggests an analogy, drawn from a special field. But the analogy is misleading, since Spengler tries to prove that all the morphological growths of civilizations conform to the same pattern, and he looks on this as a metaphysical necessity. In Whitehead's cosmology, the types of order which arise and decay depend on the dominant characteristics of the entities which build them up. There is no reason why one order should be better or worse than the last, unless perhaps we might say that, from having the opportunity of building as it were upon the ruins of its predecessors, one epoch may achieve a subtler type of order than another. In this sense, possibly, we might speak of " progress," not as a metaphysical necessity, but as made possible through the types of order in the world building upon each other.

So what are called the " laws of nature " are dominant characteristics inherited over wide societies of actual entities. They describe the prevailing ways in which actual entities objectify themselves in each other, and so are in the solidarity of one world. This fits in with the prevalent view of the laws of nature as statistical; that is to say, as average predominating characteristics of wide groups of entities. This allows for individual variation along with general uniformity within the society, and also for the laws of nature to arise and decay with cosmic epochs of the world. It also allows an interaction between the character of individual actual entities and the character of the society in which they find themselves. So actual entities reproduce the characters of the society in which they arise and which they prehend—we thus get the conformity which can be looked on both as cause and effect of the stability of types of order in nature; and we get the possibility of a new emphasis of feeling which makes for the transition to new types of order.[1]

Each society of actual entities demands the system of the Extensive Continuum in its background, but it clearly involves some of the other societies of the world more closely than others, and some so remotely for the connection to be irrelevant and negligible—for instance, societies belonging to other cosmic epochs with totally different defining characteristics. Its own so-called " causal laws " are the reproduction throughout a series of its own members of its dominant kind of feeling. So the problem of the unity of a society of actual entities becomes one of its type of organisation—perhaps we might say, a constitutional problem. By a " society " is meant a nexus of actual entities which is self-sustaining, and relatively independent of other societies.

---

[1] This interaction between the character of an actual entity and that of the society in which it arises is stated in the Categorical Obligation called " The Category of Subjective Harmony." This states that there is a harmony between the prehending subject and the data prehended. Neither can be abstracted from the other. The subject is what it is because of the data from which it arises ; but the way in which it feels them depends on its being the kind of concrescence it is. This is because all actualities are highly selective. They prehend only an infinitesimal number of all the eternal objects characterising their environment, and these with positive and negative degrees of emphasis, in accordance with their " subjective aim."

So we may talk of a star-cluster as a society; or a mountain, a forest, a man's body, a college.

We have a unity of the society as a whole. But the society only lives and acts in its members; for instance, all the life in the body is in the millions of individual cells. The " life of the body " as a whole comes from the way in which these cells are integrated together, in its "real internal constitution." So Whitehead points out that what needs explanation, the miracle of a living organism, is not dissociation, but *unified control*. We are apt to look on dissociated personality as abnormal, and as needing explanation; yet the explanation we really need is how millions of different centres of experience can be so organised that there is a unity of experience. He also points out that there are centres of reaction in the body which are not the centres of unified experience; for instance a heart can go on beating, with proper stimulants, outside the body. Worms and jellyfish are very little centralised. "The living body is a co-ordination of high grade actual occasions; but in a living body of a low type the occasions are much nearer to a democracy. In a living body of a high type there are grades of occasions so co-ordinated by their paths of inheritance through the body, that a peculiar richness of inheritance is enjoyed by various occasions in some parts of the body. Finally the brain is co-ordinated so that a peculiar richness of inheritance is enjoyed now by this and now by that part; and thus there is produced the presiding personality at that moment in the body. Owing to the delicate organisation of the body there is a returned influence, an inheritance of character derived from the presiding occasion and modifying the subsequent occasions through the rest of the body."[1] We may notice, in this notion of a "presiding personality" at any moment in the body, a view of the relation of the body and mind not far removed from that of Leibniz. The "mind" monad is that member of a group which perceives the other monads, which are called its body, most clearly. So the idea of the "interaction of mind and body" becomes the extremely general idea of a highly complex structure of actual entities in which there may be a presiding occasion which is "the final node, or intersection" of the structure, and which therefore enjoys a centralised control, a peculiar richness of inheritance from the other occasions of the nexus, and a peculiar fertility of appetition in its mental pole. This may be objectified into a succeeding "presiding occasion," in which case we can speak of a continuity of consciousness. In sleep, or illness, the control of a presiding occasion is relaxed, and the degree of centralisation in the organism is less complete.

[1] *Process and Reality*, p. 152 (166).

We may note also that since all actual entities are dipolar, the idea of a " living " body is a special form of the general idea of an enduring object, which is a genetic character inherited through an historic route of actual occasions. Some such routes form what we call inorganic material bodies. Their characteristic is unoriginality, since each new actual occasion is simply reproductive of the character of the actual occasion behind. Moreover the nexus displays an average general character, which blots out unwelcome details of deviation. Thus the character of a " material body " is simply the reiteration of the same pattern through a succession of events. But at the stage called " organic " or " living," there is some origination of conceptual feeling. This means that some elements in the environment are emphasised and objectified by the prehending occasions into themselves in a way which promotes the unified life of their structured society. An example of this would be the metabolism of food.

So it is said that primarily life comes with the origination of conceptual prehension, a novelty of appetition to match novelty of the environment. A " living " body therefore has the property of adaptability, as well as of persistence. A nexus of actual entities may be more or less living, at different periods of its historic route, or some occasions of the nexus may be living and others non-living.

But life is, in Whitehead's vivid phrase, a " clutch at novelty." We may recall the passage in *The Function of Reason*.[1] In the burning desert, a " living " organism will feel thirst and search to satisfy it; a stone will be baked and dry.

A notice of the extraordinarily subtle way in which Whitehead discusses the problem of the balance of stability and adaptability in " living " organisms, in its context of the whole question of depth of order as the right relation of narrowness and width, vagueness and definiteness, complexity of contrast and massive simplicity, must wait for our last chapters. We can only notice in passing that he shows how a progressive order is always a balance on the verge of chaos. It is to be realised, and then transcended, but not stabilised. There are times when adaptability matters more than immediate security. The originative element we call " life " comes from a sense, probably a blind sense, of an infinitude of unrealised possibilities; and this may just bring in the right new feeling which is the dawn of a new order. He develops the idea that depth or intensity of order depends on the capacity to hold together diverse elements in experience as contrasts, instead of dismissing them as incompatibilities. It is the razor edge between the dismissal of contrasts in favour of stable, if trivial, uniformity, and their

[1] P. 72.

admission at the cost of the disintegration of the organism.

It seems, on a wide view, as though the dominant types of order in societies of actual entities reached a climax, and then petered out. The organisation of the society becomes less complex, and more diffused, its defining characteristics less important.[1] The law of entropy would be an application of this.   Whitehead says that it looks as though the type of order we call the " physical " order of our cosmic epoch was wasting in this way.   But at the end both of *The Function of Reason* and of *Religion in the Making*, he throws out the suggestion, which we should like him to develop further, that in what we call " reason " the disciplined development of the originative urge of the mental pole, we may have the counter-tendency, which can build up the new type of order, which might arise out of the decay of the physical order.   Let us recall the passage in *Religion in the Making*.[2]

" The passage of time is the journey of the world towards the gathering of new ideas into actual fact.   This adventure is upwards and downwards.   Whatever ceases to ascend, fails to preserve itself and enters upon its inevitable path of decay.   It decays by transmitting its nature to slighter occasions of actuality, by reason of the

[1] *Process and Reality*, p. 49 (53-54).
[2] P. 159.

failure of the new forms to fertilize the perceptive achievements which constitute its past history. The universe shows us two aspects: on the one side it is physically wasting, on the other side it is spiritually ascending. It is thus passing with a slowness, inconceivable in our measures of time, to new creative conditions, amid which the physical world, as we at present know it, will be represented by a ripple barely to be distinguished from non-entity.

"The present type of order in the world has arisen from an unimaginable past, and it will find its grave in an unimaginable future. There remain the inexhaustible realm of abstract forms and creativity with its shifting character ever determined afresh by its own creatures, and God, upon whose wisdom all forms of order depend."

# CHAPTER VIII

## COSMIC, ETHICAL AND ÆSTHETIC ORDER IN THE "TIMÆUS" AND IN WHITEHEAD'S PHILOSOPHY

Without the Vision, the chaos of elements remains a chaos, and the Form sleeps for ever in the vast chambers of unborn designs. Yet in *that* chaos only could creative vision ever see *this* Form. Nor without the co-operant Will, obedient to the Vision, may the pattern perceived in the huddle attain objective reality.—J. L. LOWES, *The Road to Xanadu.*

THAT striking analogies can be drawn between Whitehead's cosmology (as suggested in his earlier books, such as *The Concept of Nature* and *The Principles of Natural Knowledge*) and that of the *Timæus* has been pointed out by A. E. Taylor first in his *Plato, the Man and his Work*,[1] and then in more detail in his *Commentary* on the *Timæus*.[2] All I wish to do in this chapter is to recall some

[1] Pp. 455, 456.
[2] *A Commentary on Plato's Timæus* (Oxford, 1927), Taylor's suggested analogies between the cosmology of the *Timæus* and that of Whitehead can be evaluated quite apart from the hypothesis which underlies his Commentary—namely, that the *Timæus* gives us not Plato's own views, but those of a fifth-century Pythagorean. This is a hypothesis to be estimated on its merits; it is certainly interesting and original, but is, to say the least, highly controversial. The reception it is likely to receive is perhaps indicated by the review in *Mind*,

of the interesting comparisons which Taylor draws, and try to develop his suggestions rather further as a result of the fuller data Whitehead has given us in *Process and Reality*.

Whitehead himself acknowledges[1] that the line of thought he develops in his cosmology is close to that suggested in the *Timæus*. The underlying notion in both is the view of creation as the emergence of a type of order out of a primordial indetermination.[2] Moreover, to Whitehead, as to Plato, the cause for the initial incoming of order into mere creativity is the " goodness of God," and His " choice of the best." We should not probably push this analogy too far since, as I have pointed out, to Whitehead " God " (at any rate as restricted to the context of his metaphysical system) is a strictly defined philosophical notion, whereas Plato in the *Timæus*

---

January, 1929 (by G. C. Field), and by Shorey's paper, " Recent Interpretations of the ' Timæus,' " in *Classical Philology*, October, 1928.

[1] *Process and Reality*, pp. ix, 113 (126), 129-134 (142-147).

[2] It is not relevant to Whitehead's cosmology to discuss whether Plato's view implies a belief in matter as an antecedent state of chaos out of which the world was created (which is generally stated to be the Greek view, as distinguished from the Hebrew and Christian view of creation out of nothing). The aspect of the picture given in the *Timæus* which Whitehead develops is the view of creation as the gradual incoming of a type of order where there is a general possibility of relatedness.

is speaking largely in the language of myth.   The exact place of the Demiourgos of the *Timæus* in Plato's metaphysic is a well-known problem. Perhaps Plato did not mean (some may possibly say, with Professor Shorey, that he was too wise) to give Him a defined place in a system; and it would be rash to draw too close a comparison between His creation of the universe looking to the form of the αὐτὸ ὅ ἐστι ζῷον and White-head's Primordial Nature of God as the envisage-ment of the realm of eternal objects potential for realisation in the process of creation.   But never-theless (as I suggested above) the same general idea underlies both.   The reason that there should be a " process of becoming " at all is to be looked for in the " goodness of God,"[1] that is to say, in the ultimate limitation upon mere " creati-vity " in virtue of which there can be possibilities for the rise of determinate processes; and as necessary to explain why these show a gradual approximation to more subtle types of order.[2]

---

[1] We must of course guard against too quickly drawing ethical and religious conclusions from phrases such as this. No doubt in the long run some such conclusions are justified ; but we must remember that its primary meaning was probably nearer to the Anaxagorean νοῦς—namely, the principle of order and rationality.

[2] Cf. *Timæus*, 39*d*, where the " sufficient reason " of creation is said to be ἵνα τόδ' (*i.e.* this universe) ὡς ὁμοιότατον ᾖ τῷ τελέῳ καὶ νοητῷ ζῴῳ πρὸς τὴν τῆς διαιωνίας μίμησιν φύσεως.

A. E. Taylor has pointed out the analogy between Whitehead's view of the ultimate substantial activity of nature, " passage " (or " creativity " as he calls it in *Science and the Modern World*, and in *Process and Reality*) and the doctrine of the *Timæus* of the ὑποδοχὴ γενέσεως the " matrix of becoming," which is purely indetermined potentiality, able to become determinate through the " ingression " of the forms. He well points out that we have an almost verbal parallel in *Timæus* 50c[1] to Whitehead's conception of the " passage " of nature. The identification of the ὑποδοχὴ γενέσεως with χώρα (Space), besides of course its analogy, which has been often pointed out, with the Cartesian identification of matter and extension, presents a still closer parallel to Whitehead's view of the Extensive Continuum[2] as " the most general scheme of real potentiality providing the

---

[1] *Timæus*, 50c. ἐκμαγεῖον γὰρ φύσει παντὶ κεῖται, κινούμενόν τε καὶ διασχηματιζόμενον ὑπὸ τῶν εἰσιόντων, φαίνεται δὲ δι᾽ ἐκεῖνα ἄλλοτε ἀλλοῖον· τὰ δὲ εἰσιόντα καὶ ἐξιόντα τῶν ὄντων ἀεὶ μιμήματα, τυπωθέντα ἀπ᾽ αὐτῶν τρόπον τινὰ δύσφραστον καὶ θαυμαστόν : " For it is there as a natural matrix for all things, moved and variously figured by the things that enter it, but through their agency takes on divers appearances at divers times. But the things that enter and leave are copies of the eternal things, moulded upon them in an obscure and wondrous fashion " (Taylor's translation).

[2] *Process and Reality*, Pt. II., ch. ii.

background for all other organic relations," or the " one relational complex in which all potential objectifications find their niche," which " underlies the whole world, past, present and future." But we must make two important qualifications:

(*a*) The Extensive Continuum is not merely characterless and structureless " creativity." It is characterised by general relations between events which can determine creativity and underlie the possibility for the emergence of any type of order whatsoever, and which he suggests are the relations of whole and part, overlapping and contact. " In its full generality beyond the present epoch, it does not involve shapes, dimensions and measurability; these are additional determinations of real potentiality arising from our cosmic epoch."

(*b*) We should beware of ascribing to Plato in the *Timæus* the " relational " view of Space, as defining possible and actual forms of relatedness between events, which is implied in Whitehead's view of the Extensive Continuum. I am inclined to think that Taylor, in his claim that Plato's view implies that χώρα is simply to be defined in terms of the " events " which come to pass in it, is too ready to claim that Plato has foreseen the modern view. He does however guard himself with the remark[1] that it " would be unhistorical to credit

---

[1] *Commentary*, p. 349.

either Timæus or Plato with the origination of the theory of relativity on the strength of such a coincidence." The χώρα of the *Timæus* seems to be a conception whose full generality has not yet been disentangled from what are perhaps largely empirical and mythological elements. This, however, should not make us underestimate the genius and insight of Plato's conception.[1]

The emergence of characters in the physical world needs besides χώρα, which is formless and structureless, the ὄντα or eternal objects through whose ingression it becomes characterised into a process of becoming (γένεσις). Here again

[1] It may be useful here to touch on the similar resemblance which Taylor sees between the conception of Time in the *Timæus* and modern relational views (*cf.* his Appendix to his *Commentary*, pp. 678 *sq.*, " The Concept of Time in the *Timæus* "). Here again we must beware of reading modern notions into Plato, but we may say that Taylor has well shown the fortunate insight which made Plato hold that Time came into being along with the Cosmos, and so is nothing apart from the processes of events which come to pass in it. Of course, as he well says, Plato cannot be credited with foreseeing Whitehead's view of different " slabs " of becoming, and nexūs of events involving different time systems. But his famous definition of Time as " the moving image of eternity " (εἰκὼν κινητὸς αἰῶνος), *i.e.* as a description of the way in which " eternal objects " are actualised in the process of the world of becoming, obviously suggests Whitehead's view. (See Whitehead's use of this phrase in *Process and Reality*, p. 476 [514]).

Taylor has pointed out the obvious analogy, in fact almost verbal correspondence, with Whitehead's view. He suggests moreover[1] that this view of the becoming of temporal actualities through the ingression of forms is to be connected with the view in *Philebus* 25-26, of temporal actualities as γενέσεις εἰς οὐσίαν, *i.e.* processes of development, or approximation towards a certain right proportion. He interprets this as meaning that the processes in the world of becoming are approximating to a law of structure. When they have " become," they will embody it perfectly. If this elucidation of the *Timæus* from the rather different doctrine of " becoming " in the *Philebus* is justified, we can see a still more striking analogy to Whitehead's view. To him, the whole meaning of a " process of becoming " is that it is an attempt to realise a certain " satisfaction " or " form of definiteness," and when this definiteness has been achieved, we may say that the actual entity in question has " become." Since it is then fully determinate, it answers every question about itself. This would seem to be very much the kind of view of the nature of a process of becoming suggested by Plato's phrase γένεσις εἰς οὐσίαν, and the determinate actual entity would be a γεγενημένη οὐσία.[2]

---

[1] See his note on *Timæus* 31*b* 3, and 35*b* 1-3 ; also *Plato*, p. 415.  [2] *Philebus*, 27*b*.

It is also interesting to note how, in the view of γένεσις as an " approximation to a law of structure," Whitehead and Plato (or at any rate the speaker in the *Timæus*) are akin in their interest in mathematical types of order. According to the *Timæus*, since the primæval " stuff," the ὑποδοχή, is extension, the forms of structure realised in it will be geometrical, and the speaker (according to Taylor's interpretation) is trying to go behind the four " roots " of the Ionian cosmologists, and show that the difference of the qualities of the " roots " themselves depend on their geometrical structure. In commenting on the cosmology of the *Timæus*, Whitehead finds the reason for saying that it supplements Newton's Scholium in philosophic depth in the fact that the *Timæus* " connects behaviour with the ultimate molecular characters of the actual entities," and " accounted for the sharp-cut differences between kinds of natural things by assuming an approximation of the molecules of the fundamental kinds respectively to the mathematical forms of the regular solids."[1] That is to say that he is noting with approval, and joining hands with the *Timæus* in the view suggested there, that the differences and determinations of things are the results of the dominant types of structure they display, and that these types of structure can be

[1] *Process and Reality*, pp. 131 (144), 132 (145).

reduced to simpler mathematical ratios, although of course the " higher " kinds of societies of actual entities involve more and more complex harmonies of sub-societies with interwoven structure. But this simply means that we find more and more intricate types of organisation of the simpler ratios, involving more and more complex possibilities of relatedness.

A way in which we can conceive of this " hierarchised " view of the world, as involving various orders superimposed upon each other, is suggested by A. E. Taylor in *The Faith of a Moralist*, i., pp. 360-361, in words that obviously recall Whitehead. " The whole complex pattern of the one world in which we live and have our being is made up of the most varied strands. And it is not simply a pattern with many and various strands; it is a pattern whose constitutive elements are themselves patterns, reproducing, in varying degrees of fullness and distinctness, the characteristic pattern of the whole; and this is why we can speak of the pattern of the whole as *all*-pervasive, though more clearly discernible in some of the sub-patterns than in others."

In an article on " Dr. Whitehead's Philosophy of Religion " in the *Dublin Review*, July, 1927, Taylor also approaches the interpretation of Whitehead from this point of view, and defines an organism as " a whole with a characteristic pattern of its own which repeats itself in the sub-patterns of its constituent parts."

We may again refer to Whitehead's chapter on " Rhythms " at the end of the *Principles of Natural Knowledge*. " There are gradations of rhythm. The more perfect rhythm is built upon component rhythms. A subordinate part with crystalline excess of pattern or with foggy confusion weakens the rhythm. Thus every great rhythm presupposes lesser rhythms without which it could not be."

Whitehead's view of the complexity of the cosmic order would of course differ greatly from the comparatively simple conception in the *Timæus*. But the underlying notion common to both is the view of " creation " as the gradual emergence of types of order through " peaceful penetration " by the rational, or, as it is expressed in *Timæus* 47d-48a,[1] the gradual persuasion of ἀνάγκη by

---

[1] " For indeed the generation of this our world came about from a combination of necessity with understanding, but understanding overruled necessity by persuading her to conduct the most part of the effects to the best issue ; thus, then, and on this wise was this universe compacted in the beginning by the victory of reasonable persuasion over necessity ; whence if a man would tell the tale of the making truly, he must bring the errant cause also into the story " (Taylor's translation). The force of the vivid phrase πλανωμένη αἰτία for ἀνάγκη, as the arbitrary element in things, is in some measure retained in Archer-Hind's translation " Cause Errant."

νοῦς. Taylor is surely right in interpreting ἀνάγκη here as the contingent, arbitrary element involved in the process of becoming. In Whitehead's system this, pushed as far back as it will go, would be creativity, the ultimate substantial activity, for which no reason outside itself can be given. His description of its determination through participation in the forms corresponds to the " persuasion of ἀνάγκη by νοῦς."

But here is a point which needs making clear. Whitehead quotes[1] Taylor's statement, from *Plato*, p. 455, (and the same idea appears *passim* in the *Commentary* on the *Timæus*) that " In the real world there is always, over and above ' law ', a factor of the ' simply given,' or ' brute fact,' not accounted for, and to be accepted simply as given. It is the business of science never to acquiesce in the merely given, to seek to ' explain ' it as the consequence, in virtue of rational law, of some simpler initial ' given.' But however far science may carry this procedure, it is always forced to retain *some* element of brute fact, the merely given, in its account of things. It is the presence in nature of this element of the given, this surd or irrational, as it has sometimes been called, which Timæus appears to be personifying in his language about necessity." We need to be clear here that, in speaking of " givenness,"

---

[1] *Process and Reality*, pp. 57-58 (67).

we are not making a confusion between *the nature of the subject-matter* and *the nature of our knowledge*. Taylor sometimes seems to imply by " givenness " the residue of brute fact in nature which has never been adequately analysed, though we constantly approximate to it by pushing the element of arbitrary assumption further and further back. But is not the meaning of Plato's phrase " τὸ δ᾽ αὖ δόξῃ μετ᾽ αἰσθήσεως ἀλόγου δοξαστόν, γιγνόμενον καὶ ἀπολλύμενον, ὄντως δὲ οὐδέποτε ὄν "[1] that the character of nature itself, since it is a process of becoming, and " never truly is " is such that it can never be completely known or rationalised ? This latter is undoubtedly Taylor's real view as to Plato's meaning;[2] and he is also surely right in holding that Plato's view would be that in so far as we are able to make any " likely " statements about nature, it is because it " partakes " in the order and structure of the forms. There is an excellent statement of this on p. 134 of his *Commentary*. "We have not in mere juxtaposition a scientific knowledge of the laws of number, and

---

[1] *Timæus* 28a. Quoted by Whitehead, *op. cit.*, pp. 113-114 (126).

[2] In the article in the *Dublin Review* (quoted above) he says " necessity " is the element of obstinate particularity in things. " It is always there, since we can never reduce the whole course of any concrete process to law without remainder, but it is always there as a subordinate element in a pattern which as a whole is rational."

10

also acquaintance, based on sense, with a mere chaotic jumble of 'appearances' . . . We actually do see order and regularity *in* the 'appearances.' They are what the *Philebus* calls γενέσεις εἰς οὐσίαν, and that is why we can discern laws and uniformities to which they can approximately conform, and why science can progress by looking for a preciser formula when it has found that the old one has not 'saved the appearances.'[1] It is why in cosmology, though you never pass from the 'likely story' to the exactitude of scientific finality, one 'story' can be more 'likely' than another, and why it is our duty to make our story as 'like' the truth as we can."

This exactly agrees with what Whitehead means by the intelligibility of an actual entity through its achievement of definiteness and determination in its process of becoming. It involves his view that apart from some systematic character in things, *i.e.* some way in which the world of becoming is conditioned by the general metaphysical principles which constitute the "Primordial Nature of God," there could be no possibility of understanding them, no justification

[1] There is a very interesting note on the natural history of this phrase σῴζειν τὰ φαινόμενα "to save appearances," by J. B. Mayor, in the *Journal of Philology*, vol. vi., p. 171.

Taylor (*op. cit.*, p. 60) says it means "to find a coherent expression which does full justice to the whole of the ascertained facts."

of Induction, or even of scientific measurement and observation.[1]

If, therefore, our interpretation be correct, we may perhaps sum up this discussion by saying that both Whitehead and Plato approach philosophical questions through a consideration of the nature and implications of an order in the universe. It is now time to supplement this by looking at the bearing which it has on the ethical and æsthetic sides of their philosophies.

Let us first remind ourselves that the funda-

[1] This view of systematic relatedness, and the notion of congruence, *i.e.* of identity of function within a system, is a fundamental one to Whitehead. He holds that it is prior to and presupposed in measurement, so that apart from it scientific measurement and observation are a mere subjective day dream. This is where he differs from the Einsteinian view. Einstein holds that the metrical structure of space is simply determined by physical conditions. Whitehead holds that on this view, if we are to have an adequate theory of measurement, these physical conditions must exhibit constant and general uniformities. So in order to arrive at these uniformities, he holds that physics must be rested upon metaphysics. (But *cf.* Russell's criticism, *Analysis of Matter*, p. 79, quoted *supra*, p. 209 *n*.

Possibly an analogy might here be drawn (though I should not press it too far) with Plato's discussion of measurement in *Politicus*, 283*d*. He finds, like Whitehead, the necessity of some absolute standard for measurement besides the purely relativist one of " one thing against another " (κατὰ τὴν πρὸς ἄλληλα μεγέθους) ; a standard which will be κατὰ τὴν τῆς γενέσεως ἀναγκαίαν οὐσίαν—" according to the necessary character of becoming."

mental principle — or it may be assumption —
underlying both is that the order in the world is
only explicable with reference to a primordial
limitation on mere "creativity," which is the
sufficient reason for the possibility of such order
as we find in the temporal world. This supplies
the final causation in virtue of which indeterminate
creativity is given its initial urge to become a
process of self-determination; and in so far as the
processes of the temporal world "participate" in
it, it supplies the permanent elements in virtue
of which there can be stability and solidarity in
the universe. This may be what Plato meant
by the Idea of the Good as being the sustaining
cause of all things, and their final cause as the
supreme object of rational desire.[1]  In this sense,
it is, as Taylor says,[2] "that to which the structure
of things is conceived as adapted." It may, on
the other hand, simply be the entire realm of the
Ideas. But in either case the analogy with
Whitehead's view of the Primordial Nature of
God is obvious.

But, to Whitehead, the Primordial Nature of
God, the "envisagement" of the realm of eternal
objects, or in other words, the ultimate limitation

[1] Cf. *Rep.*, 505*e*—ὁ δὴ διώκει μὲν ἅπασα ψυχὴ καὶ τούτου
ἕνεκα πάντα πράττει . . . and 509*c*.

[2] *Plato*, p. 294; and *cf.* Burnet, *Greek Philosophy*, i., p. 230
on "teleological algebra."

upon mere creativity in virtue of which there are
possibilities for the achievement of types of order,
demands for its complete actuality, or what he
calls the fulfilment of God's " Consequent Nature,"
the " ingression " of these possibilities into the
world of becoming.[1]   Whitehead therefore, in
developing the Platonic view that " the things
which are temporal arise by participation in the
things which are eternal " is able, through his view
of the " Consequent Nature of God " to do fuller
justice to the reality of the " things which are
temporal."   They do not, as Plato was tempted to
say, have a merely derivative and defective reality,
" rolling about between not being and being,"
but in so far as they participate in the eternal
objects, they actualise those eternal objects, and at
the same time partake of their nature of " everlastingness."   (Whitehead works this out in the last
part of *Process and Reality*.)

It is the doctrine of " objective immortality,"
which prevents us from taking a depreciatory view
of the temporal world.   This means that while the

[1] One might put this figuratively in the words of the *Timæus*
(34*a*), Οὗτος δὴ πᾶς ὄντος ἀεὶ λογισμὸς θεοῦ περὶ τὸν ποτὲ
ἐσόμενον θεὸν λογισθείς.   " This then was the whole thought
of the everlasting God concerning the God which was to be."
I am of course aware that the context of these words gives
them a rather different sense.   Nevertheless, we may perhaps
say that the " thought of the everlasting God " is the Primordial
Nature, the " God which is to be " the Consequent Nature.

actualities of the past have perished, the character of their "decisions" has become a "stubborn fact," qualifying the process of becoming forever, so that the heritage of the past is held in the living immediacy of the present.   This is the "Consequent Nature of God," and, according to Whitehead's development of the idea, in the last chapter of *Process and Reality*, it is to be thought of as an evolving æsthetic harmonisation, in which the quality of every passing event is held, in so far as it can be, as a contributor towards the total unity.   This is the sense in which God is spoken of as "the poet of the world."[1]

This means that to Whitehead, and here we can probably say that he is following Plato, the problems of metaphysics and of ethics and æsthetics are primarily problems concerning the nature of order, and the types of order in which processes of becoming participate.   So, to follow once more Taylor's interpretation, the reason why there is mathematical structure exemplified in nature, and the reason why there is ethical law is one and the same, since order is characteristic of the Good.   To quote him,[2] "There is a real affinity between the moral orderliness of the good life and the orderliness of the great cosmic movements, the same thought to which Kant gives a very characteristic turn in the famous closing

---

[1] *Op. cit.*, p. 490 (526).      [2] *Commentary*, p. 257.

paragraph of the *Critique of Practical Reason* about
the ' starry heaven above and the moral law within.'  The life of rule is really the ' life according
to Nature ', since the source of Nature's laws is
itself a moral one, ' God's choice of the best.' "

It has been easy for later generations to senti-
mentalise or romanticise this notion, and it is
well to remind ourselves how literal a sense it
carried in Greek philosophy.  The saying in
*Gorgias* 508 a ἡ ἰσότης ἡ γεωμετρικὴ καὶ ἐν θεοῖς
καὶ ἐν ἀνθρώποις μέγα δύναται—" Geometrical proportion has great power among gods and men "—
is an instance of its sense of the attraction, the
" fitness " of mathematical law.  The Idealist and
Romanticist tradition has carried modern philosophy far away from this kind of view, through
its concentration on the one hand on the thinking
and willing Self, and the nature of moral obligation
*per se*, and on the other hand, on the irrational
elements in æsthetic and religious experience.
So it is at first almost startling to find a modern
philosopher like Whitehead going back to what
is substantially the Platonic view.  Rational order
(as supremely exemplified in types of mathematical
structure) has a beauty and a " fitness " which to
Whitehead constitute the basis of ethical and
æsthetic order.[1]  Æsthetic order results from the

---

[1] This is not, of course, to say that beauty consists in form or
structure alone ; otherwise, as Russell points out (*Analysis of*

richness of pattern involved when intensity of contrasts is achieved concurrently with an underlying harmonisation, (*i.e.* the tension between the two extremes, of order, as mere vague uniformity, and of disorder, as involving incompatibilities and discords resolved by no " higher synthesis "). Ethical order, Whitehead holds, is derivative from æsthetic order in this sense, as the attempt on the part of actual entities to realise depth and intensity of experience without its involving mutual thwarting and incompatibilities.[1]

This is clearly an echo of the Greek view of the interrelation between the permanent elements in the nature of things as exhibiting rational order, and of our moral and æsthetic intuitions. Rationality in this sense involves both æsthetic beauty and a moral intuition of " fitness "—a complete satisfaction. Such, according to Whitehead, is the nature of God's final causation as regulating

---

*Matter*, p. 227, note), we should have to say that a musical score is as beautiful as the music which it represents. But the form or structure still remains fundamental, even though we may say that, in the whole æsthetic experience, the structure is used to convey the feeling with which it is clothed through a sensuous presentation.

[1] *Process and Reality*, pp 20-21 (23). " The antithesis between the general good and the individual interest can be abolished only when the individual is such that its interest is the general good, thus exemplifying the loss of the minor intensities in order to find them again with finer composition in a wider sweep of interest."

the course of creation—it lies in "the patient operation of the overpowering rationality of his conceptual harmonization."[1]   To those to whom, as to Plato and Whitehead, the Socratic view that " Virtue is knowledge " is interpreted as an appreciation of the satisfaction involved in a perception of the "fitness of things," either actual or possible (which is what is meant by a perception of their rationality), the criticisms which have been levelled against it, from Aristotle onwards, on the ground that λόγος οὐδὲν κινεῖ—" pure reason moves nothing "— must seem based on a fundamental misunderstanding.   We may moreover doubt whether Plato, and certainly Whitehead, ever looks at " pure reason " as something abstract and inoperative.   It is always clothed with some kind of emotional evaluation or appreciation.

We may feel that in view of the increasing complexity revealed by modern knowledge both in the physical universe and in man's psychological and social life; in view also of our tendency either to separate the moral life from the order of nature, or else to look on it as a mere instrument of biological adjustment, this idea of a kinship between man's inner life and a reason underlying nature, may seem an undue simplification.   But at the same time, it is impossible to underestimate the appeal such a view has had, since the first sug-

---

[1] *Process and Reality*, p. 490 (526).

10*

gestions, in the figurative language of Pythagorean speculation, that there was a connection between " numbers," in the cosmic rhythms and harmonies, and the events of man's life.

This view of course left its *damnosa hæreditas* on the history of thought in the speculations of astrology;[1] but it found also a noble application in passages such as *Timæus* 90*d* " To the divine part of us are akin the thoughts of revolutions " περιόδοι (cf. *supra*, p. 111) "of the All: these every man should follow . . . by learning to know the harmonies and revolutions of the All, so as to render the thinking soul like the object of its thought according to her primal nature: and when he has made it like, so shall he have fulfilment of that most excellent life that was set by the gods before mankind for time present and time to come."[2] It is therefore interesting and stimulating to find a modern philosopher like Whitehead setting forward a view which is after all not so very far removed from this, although of course his formulation of it must necessarily differ widely in its setting in the concepts of modern philosophic and scientific thought. We may not be able completely to accept Whitehead's views; but at any rate we can

[1] As has been shown by C. C. J. Webb, *Studies in the History of Natural Theology*.

[2] Archer-Hind's translation.

express our gratitude to him for such a magnificent attempt to give us a "modern form of Platonism," together with a renewal of our hope that the answer to the mystery surrounding the reason in the nature of things, and to the mystery of our ethical aspirations and æsthetic enjoyments, may lie in the same direction.

# CHAPTER IX

## FINAL APPLICATIONS OF THE PHILOSOPHY OF ORGANISM IN NATURAL THEOLOGY

Und da weiss ich, dass nichts vergeht,
keine Geste und kein Gebet,
   (dazu sind die Dinge zu schwer),
meine ganze Kindheit steht
immer um mich her.
Niemals bin ich allein.
Viele, die vor mir lebten
und fort von mir strebten,
webten,
webten
an meinem Sein.

RAINER MARIA RILKE

Bright shootes of everlastingnesse.—VAUGHAN.

It has become a commonplace to say that philosophical science today can leave room for the forms of experience not easily amenable to rational analysis; that scientific materialism need no longer be taken seriously as a metaphysic, however necessary it may be to the scientific worker as an *ad hoc* attitude towards the abstracted aspects of the world he is studying through his scientific method. Yet in view of the baffling complexity of the subject-matter; in view of the obvious inadequacy, and the dogmatic spirit which has wrecked systems of natural theology, may it not be conceded that after all the failure of that kind of thought is foredoomed ? It is an attempt to say what cannot be said; and is not Wittgenstein right in insisting that concerning that of which one cannot speak one must be silent ? (" wovon man nicht sprechen kann, darüber muss man schweigen ").[1] Had we not better leave the attempt to apply our metaphysics in the realm of ultimate questions; bow to the *mysterium tremendum*, the final incomprehensibility of the " a-logical core of the universe," while we recognise religion simply as the emotion or feeling of the numinous character of the mystery of the nature of things ? We can say that such an emotion is necessary and desirable; but we must have done with the pretentiousness and arid rationalising of philosophical theology.

This is a point of view all too common in a

---

[1] *Tractatus*, 7 ; and *cf*. F. R. Tennant, *Philosophical Theology*, vol. ii., pp. 74 *sq*. Tennant, however, like Whitehead, sees that though the World-Ground he calls God may be the " last irrationality," this does not in itself imply that we may not come to see the necessity for it by a rational process.

Cf. *Science and the Modern World*, p. 243. " For nothing, within any limited type of experience, can give intelligence to shape our ideas of any entity at the base of all actual things, unless the general character of things requires that there be such an entity."

sophisticated age which has lost God, yet feels the need of Him; and has lost hope in the possibility of a reasonable faith. There is false mysticism which is the other side of scepticism, and which, like it, is the child of despair; the mysticism, that is to say, which dares not examine the truth of its content, while scepticism knows that the search is vain.

Yet Whitehead can still hold that there is a place and a necessity for a natural theology. He is maintaining that cosmology—speculative scientific philosophy united with speculative theology—is more than fanciful myth-making. Then was not John Dewey right when he said, in his review of *Process and Reality*, that we put the book down with a feeling that the seventeenth century has got the better of the twentieth ?

Our answer cannot be given until we have genuinely tried to grasp what he is telling us. We shall never appreciate him if we start from the assumption that a rationalist philosophy must of necessity do violence to religious intuitions, before we have waited to see whether he does not also recognise those intuitions; or if (with his reviewer in *Mind*) we say that his use of " God " in his metaphysic is " scandalous," and yet can make the curious mistake of identifying his Primordial Nature of God with creativity or neutral stuff. We must have a patient understanding and appreciation of his philosophy as a whole; we must try to see what relation his "flashes of insight" bear to his general ideas; and not judge them too quickly by their congruence or incongruence with the general ideas of other religious systems.

And, in the last resort, whether we shall be willing to follow him into the realm of philosophical theology will depend upon whether we share his faith that reason is more than a chance by-product of a struggle for existence; that we may legitimately assume that "the ultimate natures of things lie together in a harmony which excludes mere arbitrariness"; that the unknowing to which we always come in the end is, as Meister Eckhart said, an unknowing beyond, and not beneath, knowing, so that rational explanation must go on being pushed to its furthest limits.

It will also depend on whether we hold that Whitehead is right in claiming that religion is more than an irrational feeling, with no significance for the ordering of life; that it inevitably issues in propositions with a bearing upon the conduct of life, and that the assumption that these are necessarily good is uncritical and directly disproved by the facts. For better or worse "your character is developed according to your faith." And so "the primary religious virtue is sincerity, a penetrating sincerity."[1]

[1] *Religion in the Making*, p. 15.

Religion is not metaphysics.  It is true that it is primarily feeling, the emotion of moments of exceptional insight, which come generally in solitude, as he well reminds our gregarious age. Yet it claims to be more than a transient, particular emotion.  It claims that its concepts " though derived primarily from special experiences, are yet of universal validity, to be applied by faith to the ordering of all experience."[1]  As soon as there is any conscious association of religion and conduct, the age of rationalism has dawned.  We must find some means of judging the value of the propositions which issue from our religion, in their bearing on " the art and theory of the inner life of man."

For " Religion," he reminds us, " is an ultimate craving to infuse into the insistent particularity of emotion that non-temporal generality which primarily belongs to conceptual thought alone. In the higher organisms the differences of tempo between the mere emotions and the conceptual experiences produce a life-tedium, unless this supreme fusion has been effected.  The two sides of the organism require a reconciliation in which emotional experiences illustrate a conceptual justification, and conceptual experiences find an emotional justification."[2]

[1]  *Religion in the Making*, p. 32.
[2]  *Process and Reality*, p. 21 (23); cf. *Religion in the Making*, pp. 31, 47.

The progressive attempt to effect this fusion is rational religion. The alternative is a philosophical scepticism together with mystical emotion; which leads on the one hand to a destructive rationalism, and on the other hand to a mysticism whose content we dare not rationalise lest we discover it to be a form of error. But this means in the end a split between our intellectual and emotional life. Instead of each enriching the other, each can only be enjoyed (as Hume saw) when the other is forgotten. How difficult it is to effect this reconciliation is not to be minimised; yet when the failure to do so becomes characteristic of the educated culture of a community, we have to fear an increasing individualism, which comes from the failure to communicate our deeper intuitions, and a lack of the zest which results from the union of thought and passion in creative endeavour.

Let us now turn to look at the way in which Whitehead finds the final applications of his metaphysic in rational religion. The difficulties are enormous; any inadequacies of his categories must here weigh in very heavily. Yet the last section of *Process and Reality* is not an *addendum* irrelevant to the rest of the book. It is an integral part of it.

We must first go back to his Category of the Ultimate—creativity. This we saw could be described as ὕλη—the pure, formless, substantial activity.   This pure activity may be opposed to the pure potentiality of the eternal objects.   But together these could have produced nothing, for "unlimited possibility and abstract creativity can procure nothing."[1]   Actuality always demands a limitation of pure creativity and pure potentiality.[2]   So for there to be any course of events whatsoever there must be a limitation upon pure creativity.   In the passage in *Science and the Modern World*[3] the ground for limitation is said to " stand among the attributes of the substantial activity."   But here there is a difficulty.   For Whitehead also insists that since all actual entities are creatures of creativity, God as an actual entity is also a creature, " the first created fact."   Creativity in itself could surely have no attributes, since an attribute is necessarily a characterisation, and all characterisation of creativity, Whitehead holds, belongs not to it in itself, but comes through its " creatures."[4]   In *Process and Reality*[5] he speaks of creativity as the " ultimate which is actual in virtue of its accidents."   By "accident" he must mean a characterisation which could be otherwise without the substantial activity itself

---

[1]  *Religion in the Making*, p. 152.

[2]  *Process and Reality*, p. 488 (523) ; *Science and the Modern World*, p. 244.

[3]  P. 249.          [4]  *Process and Reality*, p. 43 (47).

[5]  P. 9 (10).

having to be other than it is. If we can make the distinction between attribute and accident, we may say that an attribute flows from the nature of a substance, whereas an accident does not. No sufficient reason can be given in the nature of the substance for the accident being as it is; and there is thus a certain arbitrariness about it. When therefore Whitehead calls the Primordial Nature of God an " accident " of creativity, he means that we can give no reason from the nature of creativity why God is as He is, but the reason for there being any course of events at all depends on there being *some* primordial limitation upon creativity which is called God.[1] If we go on to ask how sheer creativity, itself unfettered, could

[1] The reviewer of *Science and the Modern World* (in *Mind*, October, 1926) points out that though Whitehead protests against paying "metaphysical compliments" to God, he pays Him the moral compliment of asserting that the limitation of the " ultimate irrationality " consists in His Goodness. What reason is there that the character of an ultimate limitation should be good ? Perhaps we may answer this (which is after all but a form of the age-old question whether the Good is what God wills, or God wills it because it is Good) by accepting the arbitrariness of the ultimate order, and saying that we must call it good. In His Will is our peace. Or (and I suspect this would be Whitehead's own answer), we may say that there is evidence that the elements of order in the world which in the long run prove constructive and stable are those which, as rational moral beings, we recognise as good. (*Cf.* Tennant, *Philosophical Theology*, vol. ii., pp. 110 *sq.*)

produce this primordial limitation, the answer would probably have to be that which C. G. Stone, in *The Social Contract of the Universe*, gives to the analogous question of how there can be an original creation of organisation (*i.e.* significant action in a system) by action which is not organised; when he replies that in the last resort action can do anything that it must do in order for there to be anything at all.

Turning to a more orthodox type of metaphysic, we may see a clear connection between this view of Whitehead's and the old Cosmological Argument for the existence of God, which reasons from the contingency of the world to a transcendent necessary Being. If we ask (as I have always found it tempting to do) why the world itself should not be the necessary Being, an answer is clearer in Whitehead's metaphysic than perhaps in others which have appealed to this argument. For if, with him, we take the concept of Process seriously, and hold that the creative advance of the world is a " plunge into novelty " then the world is essentially incomplete. It cannot be complete and self-consistent, or we are involved in the determinism which denies Process. If we are to hold that the temporal world is indeed a " plunge into novelty," we must say that the necessary ground of limitation transcends the temporal world, since it also provides the meta-

physical conditions of new orders of possibilities.

It may be worth while to notice in passing the
difference in this respect between Whitehead's
view and that of our other near contemporary
metaphysician, who in some ways is more like
him than any other living philosopher, namely
Professor Alexander. Alexander also does nothing if not take the idea of Process seriously.
But he tries to describe the process of the evolving
world of Space-Time without bringing in any Cosmological Argument for transcendent necessary
Being. In so doing he can only make novelty
possible by making use of the concept of Emergence; yet one is left wondering whether this
really explains anything. Can more and more
intricate organisations of Space-Time really be
effective in themselves to produce entirely new
qualities? We are having to do with a magic box
from which a great deal more can come out than
was ever put in. God, to Alexander, has to do
with new orders of possibilities. He is Space-
Time with a nisus to Deity, the next emergent
quality to which the universe strains—an ideal
new order of possibilities glimpsed over the
horizon; "the immediate object of the appetition
of the world," to use a vivid phrase of Whitehead's.
To Whitehead, He is the necessary metaphysical
ground of all possibilities whatever, both those

actualised and those waiting for actualisation, and, by reason of the Ontological Principle, Himself actual Being, and not merely an ideal.

Creativity, then, according to Whitehead, produces as a primordial fact an ordering of possibilities in virtue of which there can be the relevance of one to another in logical order, and so *some* definite character, in a course of events. This is God as the Principle of Concretion, " whereby there is a definite outcome to a situation otherwise riddled with ambiguity."[1] But we are still left wondering what he makes the precise relation between God and creativity. It is clear that they are not simply to be identified, since God as actual is limited, and creativity boundless. God, we have seen, is spoken of as the first creature, and accident of creativity. Is creativity then prior to God, as seems to be implied in speaking of God as a " creature," and of creativity as producing God ? Or is the distinction merely a logical one—*i.e.* in reality, creativity and the Primordial Nature of God are complementary sides of the same thing ?

I would suggest, tentatively as a merely amateur reader of the history of Christian Doctrine, that a very similar problem comes out in the discussions in the Greek Fathers of the relation of the First and Second Persons of the Trinity—the problem

[1] *Process and Reality*, p. 488 (523).

in fact which gave rise later to the Arian controversy. We may look on creativity as analogous to the Creative Power of the Father, and the Primordial Nature of God as analogous to the Logos—the order of a " Wisdom " in virtue of which effective creation is possible. Were these eternally together, in which case we have Origen's doctrine of the Eternal Generation of the Word ? Or should we say that " there was when the Son was not " (not, we may note, a *time* when He was not, for to the Arians, as to Whitehead, He was before the creation of the temporal world) ? The phrase πρωτότοκος πάσης κτίσεως[1] so often quoted by the Arians might be taken as almost an exact parallel to Whitehead's phrase " the primordial creature."

But if we could say that he intends the distinction of priority in creativity and the Primordial Nature to be simply a logical one, we might say that we have something not unlike the Doctrine of the Trinity in the Alexandrian Fathers. (*a*) In the first place, we have the Father as creative power; (*b*) we have the " limitation " in virtue of which God is perfect[2]; (*c*) we

---

[1] Col. i. 15.

[2] *Cf.* Bigg, *The Christian Platonists of Alexandria*, p. 198. He shows how Origen, as a Platonist, rejects the idea of God as " infinite " in the pseudo-metaphysical sense, in favour of the idea of Him as perfect, which as value necessarily implies limitation.

have the same ambiguity as there is between Origen's doctrine of the Eternal Generation of the Logos, and his Subordinationism in speaking of the Logos as a derived Deity (and so perhaps opening the way to Arianism).[1] (d) There is the interest in cosmology, in God in His relation to the world, which looks on the creator and the creation as in some way correlative. I would suggest that this interest in cosmology was characteristic of the Platonic Christianity of the Alexandrian Fathers, in contrast to the concentration on the Trinity in the Latin Fathers as a description of the nature of God alone by Himself, apart from the world and condescending to it. (e) If we rule out the Platonic, or rather Neo-Platonic dualism, and the view of matter as evil, if not illusory, which always casts its shadow on Alexandrian Christian Platonism, we might say that its view of creation is not unlike that of the Philosophy of Organism, in so far as creation is regarded as a process made possible by the incoming of the wisdom of God—a gradual becoming of order with God's immanence as the measure of its æsthetic consistency.[2] We might even suggest

[1] Cf. Bigg, op. cit., pp. 222 sq.

[2] This suggested analogy may of course be made without prejudice to the question of whether we are to hold that in any special sense Jesus of Nazareth was the Incarnate Logos, which, if I am not mistaken, is where the problem of orthodox Christianity becomes acute for our generation. I would however

that the " æons " of the Alexandrians were a mythological expression of a speculation similar to Whitehead's concerning other types of world order; whereas the perfect order would be achieved through the æsthetic harmony of God's complete immanence, when He will be " all in all." The Holy Spirit might be described as the Consequent Nature of God, as the measure of the creative order achieved in the temporal world (not, that is, the disastrous Platonic notion of an inferior deity which is the Soul of the World, but God as immanent in the creative advance of the world, and the reason for the order which makes this advance possible).

---

suggest that Thornton's use of Whitehead's Philosophy of Organism to support this, in his book *The Incarnate Lord* (London, 1928), is not really justified. He can indeed claim Whitehead's support for the view that our apprehension of the eternal order depends upon the fact of a developing incorporation of that order into the successions of events in Space-Time through an ascending cosmic series (cf. *The Incarnate Lord*, p. 98). But this has really no bearing on the Christology of the latter half of the book, since he claims that Christ is not a product of the creative organic series but an irruption of the Logos-Creator (or the absolute eternal order) into the series. See *ibid.*, p. 260. " The argument of this book can find no place for the mediator of an absolute revelation, except His metaphysical status be altogether beyond the organic series and on the level of the eternal order." It therefore in effect sacrifices the conception of an organic connection between the eternal order and the temporal series in order to preserve a finality of revelation.

I should not wish this analogy to be taken too seriously, and it is always a deceptive business to compare one system of ideas with another. It is suggested tentatively, simply as additional evidence that the questions raised are real ones. It may be of interest to see how similar problems of cosmology come up in very different settings, and how a similar kind of answer may be given. It may also serve to substantiate the claim made in Chapter V., that Whitehead's cosmology falls within the Platonic tradition. If the Platonic tradition can be purified of its suggestion of dualism, and of the illusoriness of the temporal process, and of its constant danger of slipping back into what Whitehead calls an atavistic mysticism, we may see that what is abiding in it is just this kind of view of the world as a gradual growth towards rational and æsthetic types of order, the ground for which is to be found in the fundamental nature of things.

The Primordial Nature of God then, in abstraction from creativity, Whitehead describes as the " conceptual realisation " of the whole wealth of potentiality. He further speaks of " conceptual realisation " as " envisagement " or " vision " of the eternal objects; and as a " wisdom," which orders or evaluates the realm of eternal objects.[1] This primarily, as far as we can see, must mean

[1] *Religion in the Making*, p. 160.

that the Primordial Nature of God constitutes
an order of values, which is the reason for that
" rightness in things, partially conformed to and
partially disregarded," which Whitehead says[1] is
the universal verdict of the rationalised religions
of the world.    But here the difficulties of language
are only too apparent.    For he uses words such
as " wisdom " and " vision " of the Primordial
Nature of God which, as pure conceptual experience, he says must be unconscious.    This seems
very difficult, but it follows from his view of
consciousness as arising from the integration of
mental and physical feelings.[2]    Therefore pure
mental feeling by itself would be just a formal
logical order, and, he says, unconscious.    But
as all actual entities are dipolar, God as an actual
entity cannot be looked on as fully actual when
His mental pole, *i.e.* His Primordial Nature, is
considered alone.    For besides " valuation," it
consists in " appetition," which is the urge towards
*some* realisation in physical experience which will
constitute His physical pole.    God in His Primordial Nature is God as the Unmoved Mover.    It
is unchangeable, as the complete envisagement of
the realm of eternal objects, unmoved by whatever may be the actual course of temporal events.
It does not presuppose any particular course of

[1]  *Ibid.*, p. 66.
[2]  *Process and Reality*, pp. 489 (524) and 486 (521).

events, since the events which become are self-creative, but it supplies the conditions which make *any* course of events possible.[1] Yet by attributing to it " appetition," *i.e.* the urge to become fully actual,[2] he says that it involves the becoming of *some* temporal course of events which will constitute its physical pole. By the integration of God's conceptual nature with the evolving events of the physical world, God becomes fully actual and conscious.

We might therefore say that while God starts from His mental pole, and becomes fully actual by the growth of a physical pole, the temporal world starts from orders of events in which the mental pole is almost negligible, and advances to finer and subtler types as the mental pole becomes more dominant. Why this should be so we perhaps cannot say; we can only say that empirically it appears that on the whole it is so, and refer

[1] A. E. Taylor misreads Whitehead here, in his article " Dr. Whitehead's Philosophy of Religion," in the *Dublin Review*, July, 1927. He speaks of the Primordial Nature of God as " the existence of a supreme source of limitation . . . whose all-pervading activity determines both what combinations of eternal objects shall be really possible . . . and which of these real possibilities shall in fact be actualised in the flow of events." But it is now clear that Whitehead's view does not imply the latter statement—cf. *Process and Reality*, p. 60 (70).

[2] We may recall Leibniz' use of this word ; and cf. *Process and Reality*, pp. 44-45 (48-49).

again to the answer to the not dissimilar question given in *The Social Contract of the Universe*— that the " great " enterprise of the Universe, if it is to be a " serious " enterprise starts from a condition as remote as possible from its goal, a condition namely in which there is as much incoherence and confusion as there can possibly be.

The incoming of the order of eternal objects which constitutes the Primordial Nature of God into actual occasions also provides their initial subjective aims towards development. It is the immanence of this order which alone makes any course of events possible. For "It is not the case that there is an actual world which accidentally happens to exhibit an order of nature. There is an actual world because there is an order of nature. If there were no order there would be no world."[1] That is to say, the divine element in the world is the stable element,[2] the ultimate ordering without which creativity would be mere chaos. God's Primordial Nature in itself supplies what we may say are the formal conditions of this order. Yet, as formal, it is deficient in actuality, and so Whitehead says that its valuation and appetition involve an aim towards an order as content, that is, towards the Consequent Nature,[3] which

[1] *Religion in the Making*, p. 104.    [2] *Ibid.*, p. 94.
[3] *Process and Reality*, p. 345 (373).

will be some intensity of experience. " What is inexorable in God, is valuation as an aim towards ' order '; and ' order ' means ' society ' permissive of actualities with patterned intensity of feeling arising from adjusted contrasts."

Thus God's conceptual valuation, like that of the mental pole of every actual entity, introduces creative purpose.[1] His Consequent Nature is the measure of the order attained in the evolving world. It is the order in " present immediacy," that is, in the living present, as the outcome of all the past, and as stretching forward to the unknown possibilities of the future. This is why the present is holy ground. It " holds within itself the complete sum of existence backwards and forwards, that whole amplitude of time which is eternity."[2] Since Whitehead holds that all order is, in the end, æsthetic order, he speaks of the Consequent Nature of God as the measure of the æsthetic order of the world, " the poet of the world "; and since it is also the interweaving of His Primordial Nature with the course of events, it is " the kingdom of heaven," with us today;[3] the " present immediacy of a kingdom not of this world."[4] Here we may catch a clear echo of the teaching of the great tradition of Christian Platonism.

[1] *Process and Reality*, p. 351 (380).
[2] *Aims of Education*, p. 23
[3] *Process and Reality*, p. 497 (532).     [4] *Ibid.*, p. 485 (520).

But his departure from what has been a general feature of Platonic metaphysics may be seen in the way in which he approaches the final reconciliation of what he calls the ideal opposites— permanence and flux. It will be remembered that he saw the major problem of metaphysics in the finding of a right relation between the permanent and fluent elements of the universe. Theologies and philosophies, he tells us,[1] have tended to approach the problem by conceiving a static God condescending to a fluent world, or to a world accidentally static, but which was once created out of nothing, and which shall finally pass away. Here however we have the notion of actuality with permanence requiring fluency in the temporal world as its completion, and the fluency of the actual world requiring permanence as its completion. God and the world therefore require each other, and " stand over against one another expressing the final metaphysical truth that appetitive vision and physical enjoyment have equal claim to priority in creation."[2]

The becoming of temporal actualities, for which God's Primordial Nature supplies the metaphysical conditions, the initial urge, and the relevant possibilities of order, is a process in which objective immortality means the loss of immediacy.[3] For

[1] *Process and Reality*, p. 491 (526).  [2] *Ibid.*, p. 493 (529)
[3] *Ibid.*, p. 482 (517).

time is a perpetual perishing; and when an actual entity has become, so that its achievement remains a stubborn fact, objectively immortal for other actual entities, it has perished subjectively. So both God and the world apart from one another have a deficiency. For God's conceptual nature, apart from integration with feelings derived from the temporal world, is unconscious.[1] And the evil of the temporal world, which lies deeper than any specific evil, Whitehead sees lies in its transiency (and he here lays his finger on the reason for the inadequacy of any irreligious philosophy to satisfy our most poignant need). In its passage the temporal world is a perpetual perishing; and the finer and subtler orders are the most transient, and the most precariously poised.

The obvious answer, he says,[2] to the problem of the coming into being and passing away of life in nature is the answer of Bergson's *élan vital* with its relapse into matter—

> Blow bugles, blow; set the wild echoes flying
> And answer echoes, answer, dying, dying, dying.

Yet the higher intellectual feelings, and the religious intuition of mankind, refuse to look on

[1] Whether we can accept this point depends on whether we can say that it is legitimate for Whitehead to describe a formal ordering of concepts apart from conscious mentality as a " conceptual realisation " or " envisagement."

[2] *Principles of Natural Knowledge*, p. 200.

human life as " a flash of occasional enjoyments, lighting up a mass of pain and misery, a bagatelle of transient experience."[1]  There is also, he reminds us, the greater depth of Wordsworth's answer—

> The music in my heart I bore
> Long after it was heard no more.

If we can look on such consistency as is achieved in the self-creative advance of the temporal world as the immanence of God in the world, we can then see how the twofold deficiency arising from the opposition of God and the world may be overcome.  For in the Consequent Nature of God, God's conceptual feelings become conscious from integration with His physical feelings of each actuality as it arises; and that actuality contributes the quality of its own objective immortality to the progressive æsthetic harmonisation which is the immediacy of God's experience of the temporal world.  He holds the actual entities of the past as objectively immortal in the immediacy of His own nature, somewhat as in memory the present actual occasion knows itself as arising from its past occasions, the quality of which it holds as contributors to its own nature.[2]  We have here the notion of " everlastingness " which Whitehead says is " the content of that vision upon which

---

[1] *Science and the Modern World*, p. 268.
[2] *Process and Reality*, p. 496 (531-532).

the finer religions are built "[1] and by which, he says, is meant the combination of permanence with living immediacy. So God " does not create the world," for the actualities of the world are themselves processes of self-creation. But in His Consequent Nature, He " saves the world as it passes into the immediacy of His own life."[2] We may conceive of this " operative growth of God's nature " under the image of " a tender care that nothing be lost." Here, as a testimony to the deep significance of this idea, we may recall the philosophy of religion of a thinker of a very different school, the late Professor Höffding's view of religion as a faith in the conservation of values.

This is why actuality is haunted by the sense of worth beyond itself.[3] For it contributes its quality to God's Consequent Nature. Hence this same quality may be " redeemer or goddess of mischief."[4] For there is an inexorableness in creative advance, in which objective immortality constitutes stubborn fact which cannot be evaded. And while we may say that the immanence of God is the measure of the æsthetic consistency of the world, the societies of actual entities of the world show also lack of consistency, and mutual thwarting. We have some stability, some creative order in virtue of the divine element

---

[1] *Process and Reality,* p. 492 (527).
[2] *Ibid.,* p. 490 (525-526).       [3] *Ibid.,* p. 495 (531).
[4] *Ibid.,* p. 497 (533).

in the world, but it is precariously poised amid chaos, in which the temporal world is seen to be not so much æsthetic order as a maze of cross purposes. This is why the complacent optimism of the natural theology based on the old form of the Teleological Argument is doomed to failure. Lucretius long ago, and Hume after him in his *Dialogues concerning Natural Religion*, showed that if this be the last word,

> Nequaquam nobis divinitus esse paratam
> Naturam rerum : tanta stat prædita culpa.[1]

Yet without some measure of creative order there could be no stability and no possibility of effective advance into novelty. So, besides the maze of cross purposes, there is the æsthetic harmonisation of such order as is achieved in the temporal world. Here again we see that it is probably true to say that Whitehead's view is derived not so much from its thinking about physics, or even ethics, as about æsthetics. Or in other words, for him all order is in the last resort æsthetic order.[2] By æsthetic order he means some synthesis of contrasts—an identity and difference which makes possible some degree of intensity of feeling. And since some degree

---

[1] *De Rer. Nat.*, v., 198, 199.
[2] *Religion in the Making*, p. 105.

of intensity is the common denominator of all acts of experience, an act of experience is called an æsthetic fact. The concrescence of actual entities exhibits some æsthetic order. This is more than just system, or pattern in the sense of mere repetition, since each phase brings a new synthesis of contrasts, so we have " order entering upon novelty."[1]

He traces, with what we must feel is an extraordinary subtlety and penetration, the conditions for intensity and depth of æsthetic order. Such depth in intensity comes always from the razoredge balance between narrowness and width, definiteness and vagueness.

Triviality " arises from excess of incompatible differentiation ";[2] and also from the uniformity of a too stabilised order in which the possibility of effective contrast is excluded. " Some narrow concentration on a limited set of effects is essential for depth "; and yet at the same time " the right chaos, and the right vagueness, are jointly required for any effective harmony."[3] For only so do we achieve the " massive simplicity " which is the background of an effective order, and which secures the blotting out

[1] *Process and Reality*, pp. 480 (515), 394-395 (425-426). *Religion in the Making*, ch. iii., § 7.

[2] *Process and Reality*, p. 156 (170).

[3] *Ibid.*, p. 157 (171).

of irrelevant detail. He dwells also[1] on "the contrast between order as the condition for excellence, and order as stifling the freshness of living," and shows how just the concept of order in itself is not enough. For "it seems as though the last delicacies of feeling require some element of novelty to relieve their massive inheritance from bygone system. Order is not sufficient. What is required is something much more complex. It is order entering upon novelty; so that the massiveness of order does not degenerate into mere repetition; and so that the novelty is always reflected upon a background of system." We may meditate on passages such as this, in their application to the order which may be expressed by a picture, a poem, a government, a man's character and his life-interests. Perhaps, if such an example is permitted we may see a supreme exemplification of these principles of the depth and intensity of order in the parables of the New Testament. There is the "massive simplicity" of the background, the facts of the world seen in relation to the Father who loves righteousness and mercy; the narrowness and depth of concentration on the little world of Galilee; and the vivid realism with which the relations of men good and bad are seen with the immeasurable innocence, which, as Whitehead

[1] *Ibid.*, pp. 479-480 (514-515).

says, is a "rationalism derived from direct intuition and divorced from dialectics."[1] So they remain, a sword-thrust into the heart of life, their penetrating paradoxes and contrasts still speaking with an authority greater than that of the successive generations of scribes who have tried to trivialise them into workable platitudes.

But there is another aspect of the æsthetic order of the world which forbids the complacent optimism of eighteenth century natural theology—the "jaunty assurance" of a Pope or a Paley. For the evil in the world lies in the characters of things being mutually obstructive; organisms must prey upon one another; and the idea that the most valuable have the greatest survival value is in plain contradiction to the facts. Instead, it is the organisms with deeper and subtler types of order which are the most precariously poised, and whose life is the most transient. For novelty and freedom may be won at the expense of the stability of an order perfectly adapted to a particular form of environment. So the society of molecules composing a rock may have a survival value of hundreds of millions of years, those composing a man's life of only 70 years.[2] The transiency of the subtler types of order, the mutual obstructiveness in the characters of organisms,

---

[1] *Religion in the Making*, p. 57.
[2] *Symbolism*, p. 76.

are facts of evil in the world which Whitehead's philosophy does not burk. But he also claims that we have evidence that the final underlying order of the world is a moral order (the divine order whose self-limitation is the exclusion of evil).[1] For evil is unstable; "the common character of all evil is that there is some concurrent realisation of a purpose towards elimination." That is to say, while evil is positive, it is also destructive, and in the end self-destructive. This may not mean gain in progress (in fact evil may definitely hold up creative progress unless it be made an opportunity for eliciting greater good) for " the evil in itself leads to the world losing forms of attainment in which that evil manifests itself. Either the species ceases to exist, or it sinks back into a stage in which it ranks below the possibility of that form of evil." So evil may involve degradation, in which the evil exists in virtue of comparison with what might have been. A hog is not an evil beast; but when a man is degraded to the level of a hog there is evil. The instability which leads to the elimination of a form of evil may result in extinction for the species, in the atrophy of the finer feelings which make a comparison with what might be possible, or in the overcoming of the evil through the development of a yet more subtle order in which

[1] *Religion in the Making*, p. 95.

even the evil facts also are turned to good account. For Whitehead reminds us that there is also the notion of redemption through suffering, which haunts the world.[1] And he suggests that this is how the world is saved in the final harmonisation of God's Consequent Nature.[2] His Consequent Nature is the positive construction of value out of the wreckage of the temporal world. So what is positive and constructive is so far good. For " there is a self-preservation in that which is good in itself. Its destruction may come from without but not from within."[3]

The purpose of the divine order is the positive attainment of value; for there is a quality of life beyond the mere facts of life.[4] So the final question the spirit asks is, " What in the way of value is the attainment of life ? And it can find no such value till it has merged its individual claim with that of the objective universe. Religion is world-loyalty."

For we recall the description of a process of becoming as a subjective aim towards " satisfaction."——the attainment by an actuality of its own definiteness. And it may have sounded as though we had here simply a metaphysic which reflects

---

[1] *Process and Reality*, p. 495 (531).
[2] *Ibid.*, p. 315 (341).
[3] *Religion in the Making*, p. 98.
[4] *Ibid.*, pp. 60 and 80.

the catch-words of the age, of self-realisation and self-expression. This indeed is an image under which we might rightly conceive the nature of a process of becoming without religion. For the Philosophy of Organism holds that, besides the value of the community of individuals interrelated to one another, there is the value of the individual alone in itself. But religion begins when the individual realises the terrifying fact of its solitariness in the face of the whole vast scheme of things, and the fact that it has some unique responsibility towards it. Then, Whitehead says, it may pass through three stages, in the transition from God the void to God the enemy, and from God the enemy to God the companion.[1]

The last stage is reached when it merges its individual value with the claim of the divine order in the world. For " the antithesis between the general good and the individual interest can be abolished only when the individual is such that its interest is the general good, thus exemplifying the loss of the minor intensities in order to find them again with finer composition in a wider sweep of interest."[2] And God in the world " is that element in virtue of which our purposes extend beyond values for ourselves to values for others. He is that element in virtue of which the attainment

---

[1] *Religion in the Making*, p. 16.
[2] *Process and Reality*, p. 21 (23).

of such a value for others transforms itself into value for ourselves."[1]

So the incarnation of God in the world is both the measure of such æsthetic order as is to be found, and the reason for the value of existence in actualising this order. And religion is loyalty to the divine order; both in its conservation of values here in present immediacy, and as the creative, imaginative grasp of orders of possibilities which might be——" the perpetual vision of the road which leads to the deeper realities."[2] It is the knowledge of a kingdom of heaven with us today, an order in which objective immortality does not mean transiency and loss.

It is an order which may be disregarded; for it is never force. God's power lies above the sphere of competitive forces, the world of claims and counter-claims; " it lies in the patient operation of the overpowering rationality of His conceptual harmonisation."[3] The divine reasonableness which gives the creative solution to each situation never thrusts itself upon us. As Professor Hocking says[4] " Anger pitted against anger can never be sure of conquest: but a ' soft answer ' enters

[1] *Religion in the Making*, p. 158.

[2] *Ibid.*

[3] *Process and Reality*, p. 490 (526) ; cf. *Science and the Modern World*, p. 268.

[4] *The Meaning of God in Human Experience* (Yale, 1912), pp. 221-222.

the situation as a new idea. If it conquers it is because, refusing to compete, it *includes* and itself stands outside the arena. Without further illustration, may I suggest the principle that the supreme power in every case is a non-competing power, one which may seem at first glance even irrelevant to the point at issue. . . . The authentic voice of God, if it is to come to man with a wholly irresistible might of meaning, must be a still, small voice."

# CHAPTER X

## CONCLUSION

Οὐ γὰρ περὶ τοῦ ἐπιτυχόντος ὁ λόγος, ἀλλὰ περὶ τοῦ ὅντινα τρόπον χρὴ ζῆν.—PLATO : *Rep.* 352*d.*

IN the preceding chapters I have been trying to bring into relief some of the main features of the Philosophy of Organism. Once more let it be said, this book is not intended to be an epitome of Whitehead's great work. It is, as I said at the outset, of the nature of an acknowledgment of the interest which a student has found in it; and an interpretation which is necessarily made from the humanist and not from the scientific point of view. In these concluding pages, I should like it to recall a few of the leading ideas which we have found in the Philosophy of Organism which, when they are lived with, may be found to have a significance beyond their theoretical interest.

In the first place, there are the implications of taking the idea of Process seriously. The substitution of the concept of the " event " for that of " Substance " means that the nature of things is essentially a happening. This was the dominant note in Whitehead's earlier *Naturphilosophie.*

The new development in what he has called his Philosophy of Organism is, I take it, the elaboration of the concept of the event into that of the concrescence. This means that we take seriously not only the concept of Process, but also that of Growth. The very being of things consists in their process of concrescence — their being a growth into a new unity. We have no longer the materialist concept of an enduring stuff, whose apparent configurations lead us into an illusory belief in change and growth. Whitehead (like Bergson and Alexander) sees that growth and creative process must be taken as fundamental.

And Whitehead, through his use of the concepts of Periodicity and Rhythm, shows that the distinctions in what we call Mechanism and Life are distinctions not of categories of being, but of the character of the process. Where a process shows mere repetition and reproduction of its character, we have a mechanical type of order; where we have the increased sensitivity which brings about a continual re-creation of the character of the organism in response to new conditions and possibilities in the environment, we have a " living " type of order. The originative urge towards this increase in sensitivity is the " mental pole "; and there is no level in the whole creative process at which we can confidently say that it is absent.

So we have a renewal of the Platonic view of a kinship between natural, moral and æsthetic law; a relation between the creative order in nature and æsthetic beauty of form.

There is a book waiting to be written by someone who is both a musician and a philosopher to show that the Greek conception of the " music of the spheres " was not mere mythology. We have the concept of periodic vibrations and rhythmic repetitions in nature; of Life as the emergence of a new form supervening upon a background of ordered repetition; the principle of " resonance "[1] by which the period of one vibration is tuned to that of another so that a small expenditure of energy may achieve far-reaching results, as when the touch of a finger, in tune with its oscillations, releases a giant rocking stone. In all such principles, may we not be gradually uncovering a formal structure in things which in one case we formulate mathematically, in another reproduce and develop through significant sound in music ?[2] The relation between the formal element in things and the concrete things themselves may be analogous to the relation between the formal structure of a melody and its sensuous expression through a medium in such a way as to

---

[1] *Introduction to Mathematics*, pp. 170-171.

[2] *Cf.* the definition of Music as the art of creating significant forms in sound in Sir Henry Hadow's *Music* (H.U.L.), p. 19.

convey depth of feeling and intellectual enjoyment.

If what we call " law " consists in the achievement and displaying of some ordered character throughout the flux of events, then progress in creative advance depends upon the continual achievement of deeper and subtler orders. And depth of order, in nature, in æsthetics, in ethics is a matter of the right combination of a background of massive simplicity with a foreground of intensity and delicacy of mutually adjusted contrasts. In creative advance each order is to be achieved and then transcended. Mere repetition and routine, and contentment with what has been means mechanism. Life depends on the continual re-creation which comes from increased sensitivity and from being awake to respond to finer and subtler possibilities.

If we can hold that these possibilities are grounded in a permanent source of order, and their gradual achievement in the passage of nature is the immanence of that order in the world, we need not be troubled by the false antithesis of dualism between God and the world. The Divine Order is found both in the order of logic, which provides the necessary conditions for events to occur at all, and which " lies upon the universe as an iron necessity,"[1] and in the æsthetic order,

[1] *Science and the Modern World*, p. 27.

which " stands before it as a living ideal moulding the general flux in its broken progress towards finer, and subtler issues."

The Consequent Nature of God is the measure of such order as has been achieved in the creative passage of nature. It is that order in present immediacy. This insistent note of " present immediacy " is the answer to those who would argue that a preoccupation with speculative metaphysics must necessarily destroy interest in the vivid immediacy of life. For the conception of the Consequent Nature of God, and indeed of the concrescent actual entity, mean nothing if they do not point us to the present as that creative moment in the passage of nature which is indeed all that there is.

But the present moment is all that there is because it holds within itself the impact of the whole past from which it arises; and it reaches forward to the unknown possibilities of the future. Hence it is holy ground. There can be no substitute for its precious uniqueness, or for the sensitivity which penetrates to the bottom of each new experience as it arises. Yet we have here not simply an Epicurean *Carpe diem*. For according to the Philosophy of Organism, each present experience is not simply a detached and passing event, but the Whole found in a new unity.

Mich hat nicht *eine* Mutter geboren.
Tausend Mütter haben
an den kränklichen Knaben
die tausend Leben verloren,
die sie ihm gaben.[1]

Each experience is the outcome of a feeling of the whole of the rest of its world. It is the many gathered up into a new unity.

So if, in Whitehead's language, the individual concrescence arises out of its prehensions of the rest of its world, we can no longer hold to another old antithesis—that between egoism and altruism. For if we think of ourselves as arising out of our relations with others, we finally come to think of our good as identified with theirs.

Yet this is not the familiar metaphysic in which the individual becomes submerged and lost in the Whole. For here again the Philosophy of Organism saves itself by taking the ideas of growth and process seriously. Each individual concrescence is part of a whole process which is essentially a plunge into novelty. It is the outcome of the past; but it also reaches forward into the possibilities of the future. It arises out of its feelings of the rest of its world; but it is itself a new concrescence, with its own unique quality and value. Hegelian Monism overlooked this private and

[1] Rainer Maria Rilke, *Frühe Gedichte*. The quotation at the beginning of Chapter IX is also taken from this book.

unique side of each actuality. (We may recall the quotation from William James *On Some Hegelisms*, which I have set at the beginning of Chapter IV.) It is this which the Philosophy of Organism is concerned to restore. And it is in the responsibility which comes from the unique value of the individual actuality, alone by itself, that we first find the necessity of religion. Hence the saying (so often quoted, and so often mis-quoted) that "Religion is what the individual does with his own solitariness."[1]

Lastly, Whitehead, like all great philosophers, shows us the falsity of another famous antithesis. He shows us that there need be no final separation between the spirit of rationalism and of roman-ticism. He teaches us the zest for living as more than philosophising; and the love of philosophy as an enrichment of life. Exact reasoning is to be prized, since it is in truth the "fittest"; yet it need never destroy the immediate enjoy-ment of concrete experience. Rationality, in the broadest sense, we may call the power of discerning the order relevant to each experience. It is thus more than mere calculating, for it contains also the immediacy of æsthetic appreciation.

We need to recover this balance, in view of the tendency on the one hand to a type of learnedness which stifles the vividness of living; and on the

[1] *Religion in the Making*, p. 16.

other hand to a depreciation of attempts at exact thinking. It is this sort of wisdom and balance which runs through Whitehead's books, and for which alone we should be grateful to him, whether or no we think that he has proved his case for speculative philosophy. We may certainly feel that if we are to have speculative philosophy, there are few whom we should equally trust to give it to us. Nor can it be denied that his own particular system, which he would be the last to claim as final, has nevertheless considerable application. For penetrating general ideas have been born from it, which illuminate the experience in which we seek to test them.

But it is as a defence of the right kind of rationalism rather than for any particular metaphysical views that we would judge his work is likely to be of the most permanent significance. He would not claim to be giving a complete answer to the problems of metaphysics; but to be trying to raise the right sort of ulterior questions and to be suggesting a method by which they may be approached.[1] And by the way in which he does this, he renews our loyalty, instead of what might be our paralysing fear, in the face of our ignorance of the nature of things. He does not pander to our psychological craving for certainty in a baffling world, nor give us a " philosophy of noble

[1] Cf. *Principles of Natural Knowledge*, p. viii.

despair." But he strengthens our grounds for be-lieving that there is a positive and constructive order in things; and renews our hope that in quiet reason-able love, working without haste and without rest, is the divine life of the world.

So finally, he teaches us to hold our particular metaphysical view lightly, knowing that it is at best but a world-myth; yet not to give way to the anti-intellectualism which refuses to allow that the philosophical quest is worth pursuing.

# INDEX OF PROPER NAMES

283

# GENERAL INDEX